WORKS ON VISION

The Library of Liberal Arts
OSKAR PIEST, FOUNDER

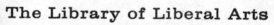The Library of Liberal Arts

WORKS ON VISION

GEORGE BERKELEY

Edited, with a commentary, by
COLIN MURRAY TURBAYNE
Professor of Philosophy, University of Rochester

· ·

The Library of Liberal Arts
published by

THE **BOBBS-MERRILL** COMPANY, INC.
A SUBSIDIARY OF HOWARD W. SAMS & CO., INC.
Publishers • INDIANAPOLIS • NEW YORK

George Berkeley: 1685-1753

A TREATISE CONCERNING THE PRINCIPLES OF HUMAN
KNOWLEDGE was originally published in 1710

AN ESSAY TOWARDS A NEW THEORY OF VISION was
originally published in 1709

ALCIPHRON was originally published in 1732

THE THEORY OF VISION, OR VISUAL LANGUAGE
VINDICATED AND EXPLAINED was originally published
in 1733

CONTENTS
· · · · · · · · · · · · · · · ·

WORKS ON VISION

The Theory of Vision, or Visual Language
Vindicated and Explained

COMMENTARY [1]

1. THE THREE ACCOUNTS AND AN OUTLINE

Berkeley's three accounts of vision—the *Essay*, the account given in the fourth dialogue of *Alciphron*, and *Visual Language*—are presented here, for the first time, in one volume. To these I have prefaced Berkeley's summary of the theory from his *Principles*.

Berkeley never lost his love for the child of his youth, his new theory of vision. He presented it to the public in three different styles and on ten different occasions during his life, thereby outdoing the seven editions of his own single best seller, *Siris*. He published the *Essay* five times, twice by itself, in 1709 and 1710, and three times in 1732 as an appendix to *Alciphron*. *Alciphron* went into four editions, the last appearing in 1752 without the *Essay* as an appendix. He published *Visual Language* only once, in 1733.

The appearance of these three accounts in one volume is felicitous, for they are stylistically complementary. To my knowledge, no other major work has been presented by its author first in the analytical or inductive style, then in the synthetical or deductive style, and finally in dialogue form. The present edition is comparable to including, in one volume, not only Newton's *Opticks*, Part I, but also his projected but never written Part II, with the same material presented deductively, and, in addition, a Part III rendered into dialogue. It is like having not only Euclid's *Optics* but also two

[1] The interpretation given here is by no means the generally accepted one. For reference to other, more traditional ways of viewing these works, see the Selected Bibliography, p. xlvii. Much of the material contained in this commentary is developed more fully in my recent book, *The Myth of Metaphor* (New Haven and London: Yale University Press, 1962).—I am indebted to my colleagues, Professors Lewis White Beck and John Stewart, for their valued comments on the first draft of this Commentary.

other works, now lost or never written, with the same material presented inductively and in dialogue.

In giving his account Berkeley uses two procedures formulated by Plato. Adopted by subsequent scientists including Berkeley's teacher, Newton, they are, after modifications, still used. Traditionally called, in Greek, analysis and synthesis, and, in Latin, resolution and composition, they are now called the method of scientific discovery and the axiomatic method. These names mark "the difference," in the words of Aristotle between "arguments *to* and those *from* the first principles," [2] respectively.

The *Essay*, like Newton's *Opticks*, is offered as a work in scientific discovery. As its title indicates, Berkeley does not yet present his theory; it is "an essay *towards* a new theory." What, then, is the principle towards which he argues? It is the astonishing conclusion that the proper objects of vision form a language. Always the tactician, apparently he thought it more prudent to end with the shocker than to begin with it; hence, the analytical or inductive style. The language metaphor, submerged throughout, is brought to the surface only at the conclusion. But Berkeley quietly insinuates its power by using language as a simile on several occasions. Visual data suggest physical objects to us *just as* the words of an ordinary language suggest their meanings. But the linguistic vocabulary of "sign," "signify," "thing signified," etc., is absent from this work.

On the other hand, *The Theory of Vision or Visual Language . . . Vindicated and Explained,* like Euclid's *Optics,* is set down deductively. As its title indicates, Berkeley now presents his theory. It is an argument *from* his principle: ". . . in the synthetical method of delivering science . . . ," he says, "we proceed in an inverted order, the conclusions in the analysis being assumed as principles in the synthesis. . . . from thence deducing theorems and solutions of phenomena." [3] Nevertheless, it was never Berkeley's practice to present his deductive systems in the dry, strigose way of Euclid and Newton. It is

2 *Nicomachean Ethics* 1095a.
3 *Visual Language*, sec. 38.

left to the reader to separate the several scholia from the theorems, and the postulates from the definitions. Vision is now described as the interpretation of just another language sharing many of the features of an ordinary language like English or French. Berkeley's previous account of vision is transformed. Having concluded that the proper objects of vision form a language, he provides himself with the new vocabulary that, previously, he had no right to use. The linguistic idioms of "sign," "thing signified," etc., are here used with great confidence but still sparingly. The *Essay* can now be rewritten, and so perhaps can the *Principles*. After answering his critic of the *Daily Post-Boy*, Berkeley presents his theory in thirty tersely written paragraphs.

A year earlier, in *Alciphron*, Berkeley presented the account even more briefly, in the same sequence as that of *Visual Language*. There are, however, important additions for which students may be grateful.

I should like to exhibit one skeleton of the three accounts, using my own terms in order to bring to the surface some of the partially submerged features of Berkeley's language metaphor. Thus, by substituting "words" for "proper objects of sight," "referents" for "tactual objects," "Principle of Ostensive Definition" for "Principle of Association," etc., the solution of a problem in optics is transformed into that of a problem in linguistics. I shall amplify the relevance of these substitutions in sections 6 and 7 of this commentary. The skeleton, read from top to bottom, shows roughly the theory of vision, that is, the deductive sequence of the argument of *Visual Language*. Inverted, it shows roughly the argument towards the theory presented in the *Essay*. The crucial experiment (7) performed on the congenitally blind, designed to test "the pillar" of the theory (2), is referred to, as are three other experiments (in 3, 4, and 5) designed to test the three important theorems that explain three well-known cases of illusion. The references to Berkeley's works are by section numbers.

2. LANGUAGE OR THE MACHINE?

Why did Berkeley try so hard to impress on his audience the point made in his new theory of vision? Ostensibly his theory was designed to solve the ancient problem of how we see, but Berkeley had purposes ulterior to this.

In his last work, the *Principles of Philosophy* (1644), Descartes summarized his life's work: "I have hitherto described the earth and generally the whole visible universe *as if* it were merely a machine in which there was nothing at all to consider except the shape and movement of its parts." [1] A hundred years later, Berkeley might have summarized his work in similar fashion: "I have hitherto described the earth and generally the whole visible universe *as if* it were merely a language in which there was nothing at all to consider except its words and their meanings and the rules of its grammar." In his last book, *Siris* (1744), he wrote: "The phenomena of nature, which strike on the senses and are understood by the mind, form not only a magnificent spectacle, but also a most coherent, entertaining, and instructive discourse; and to effect this, they are conducted, adjusted, and ranged by the greatest wisdom. This language or discourse is studied with different attention and interpreted with different degrees of skill. But so far as men have studied and remarked its rules, and can interpret right, so far they may be said to be knowing its nature." [2]

Descartes' "giant clockwork of nature" and Berkeley's "universal language of nature" identify two opposing world-views, one of which is well known, the other not, and, correspondingly, two opposing metaphors or models, one of which has been used with enormous success in the sciences, and the other, barely tried. I mean by "metaphor" the presentation of

[1] *Principles of Philosophy*, IV. 188, from *The Method, Meditations and Selections from the Principles of Descartes*, tr. J. Veitch (14th edn.; Edinburgh and London, 1907).

[2] *Siris*, sec. 254.

facts belonging to one sort in idioms appropriate to another, or the representation of facts *as if* they belonged to one sort when they actually belong to another.[3] If a metaphor is extended and its features specified, we have what I shall call a "model." Because Descartes and Berkeley presented facts in the idioms appropriate to machines and language, respectively, and spelled out the features of machines and language that they needed, we can say (although they never did) that they were using models.

Descartes envisaged the application of the mechanical model to almost every subject, and actually did use it to solve problems in physics, optics, physiology, and psychology. For example, he treated the bodies of men and dogs as "earthly machines," and emotions like love and hate as the effects of "some movement of the animal spirits." In all this he was a successful innovator; his student, Newton, exhibited the power of the machine in physics, and the mechanical model still dominates all others used in science. Realizing Descartes' dream, it dominates all other illustrations of the physical world, including the world of living things. In biology, mechanism has elbowed out vitalism and neo-vitalism, and now elbows out emergence. The time is even imminent when a neo-Cartesian may exclaim: "Give me extension and motion and I will construct life!" But now it begins to dominate earlier rival illustrations of the human mind.

Berkeley may have designed a similarly wide application of the linguistic model; unlike Descartes, he did not carry out his design. Instead, he devoted his main effort to the direct attempt to explode the myth of mechanism. In the words of his wife, "had he built as he has pulled down, he had been a master builder indeed; but unto every man his work: some must remove rubbish, and others lay foundations. . . ."[4] Had

3 My definition of "metaphor" is much the same as Gilbert Ryle's definition of "category-mistake." See his *The Concept of Mind* (London: Hutchinson's University Library, 1949), pp. 8, 16.

4 Letter from Mrs. Anne Berkeley to her son, in *The Works of George Berkeley, Bishop of Cloyne*, ed. A. A. Luce and T. E. Jessop (Edinburgh: Thomas Nelson, 1948-57), VII, 388.

he been, like his great rival, a creative trespasser instead of a prosecutor, and applied language to as many subjects as Descartes applied the machine, we might now be living in a different world.

Nevertheless, he did try to paint, but only with a broad brush, an alternative picture. For the hidden causes in the giant clockwork, acting of necessity to produce their effects according to the laws of its mechanism, known as the laws of nature, he substituted the observable signs of a universal language which may suggest things signified without any necessity but nevertheless fairly regularly, that is, according to the rules of its grammar. For the supreme mechanic, a "distant deity" hardly needed any more (the clock being automotive), he substituted the author of a language, an "immediate presence" whose message we can "hear" with our eyes. But in all this he failed. His attempt to persuade the scientists of his day to accept his reallocation of the same facts was vain. In the words of Whitehead, "he failed to affect the main stream of scientific thought. It flowed on as if he had never written." [5] Perhaps he failed because, unlike Descartes, he had chosen a weak metaphor lacking the illuminating power of the machine. But this is doubtful. He failed, more likely, because he never applied his metaphor to various subjects in detail.

He did, however, use language as a model to illuminate just one subject in detail. His essay on vision was the first of his many attempts to explode the Cartesian-Newtonian myth. It was also his first attempt to insinuate an alternative one. He did this by setting language against the father of the machine, namely, geometry, in an attempt to solve the problem of vision, a subject that had been dogmatically illustrated by geometry for over two thousand years. He tried to show that the linguistic model peculiarly illuminates this ancient problem of how we see, and that it sheds a bright light on dark areas only dimly lit by its great rival. In this way Berkeley's account of vision fitted into his "entire scheme." He was try-

5 Alfred North Whitehead, *Science and the Modern World* (Cambridge: Cambridge University Press, 1926), p. 83.

ing to refute Cartesian and Newtonian mechanism in just one subject. He was trying to refute mechanism by refuting geometrical optics considered not as a set of rules for fulfilling its ulterior design—specifically, the making of lenses and mirrors—but as an explanation of how we see. He was offering a rival theory of vision.

3. THE SIGNIFICANCE OF BERKELEY'S NEW THEORY

Berkeley's theory of vision has a still richer significance today. This makes it hard to classify. It straddles so many fields that, like Plato's *Republic*, it does not fit readily into any well-known category of philosophical or scientific writing.

It is, for example, a work in the science of optics, an attempt to shake the foundations, laid down by Kepler, of geometrical optics considered as a theory of vision—an attempt currently being made again by Vasco Ronchi.[1] In this respect it is the first argument in the classical debate between nativism and empiricism in optics, nativists holding and empiricists denying that we have direct or immediate visual perception of the three dimensions of space. It is thus the first work in physiological optics, a discipline only named and defined a century and a half later, by Helmholtz. In this respect also it is the first work to make full use of the principle of association, the later use of which entitled Berkeley's great student, David Hume, to (as Hume said) "so glorious a name as that of an 'inventor.'"[2]

Berkeley's theory of vision is the modern member of the trio of great philosophical classics written on the problem of our perception of the external world, the other two being Plato's *Theaetetus* and Aristotle's *De Anima*. Berkeley's work is the

[1] *Optics: The Science of Vision* (New York: New York University Press, 1957), tr. Edward Rosen from *L'Ottica scienza della visione* (Bologna, 1955).

[2] David Hume, *An Abstract of A Treatise of Human Nature* (1740), in *An Inquiry Concerning Human Understanding*, "Library of Liberal Arts," No. 49 (New York, 1955), p. 198.

first attempt to demolish a well-known sense-datum theory, the Theory of Representative Perception, or the Copy or Causal Theory, according to which the external world is known to us only by inference; whenever we see or otherwise perceive material things, we work back to the start of a causal sequence from the other end, the effects in us, our own private sense data or ideas. Complementally, it is the first systematic presentation of the basis of an alternative and more controversial sense-datum theory according to which the external world is intimately known to us; whenever we see or otherwise perceive, we are directly acquainted with material things, for these are nothing but combinations of sense data or ideas. "Thus, for example, a certain color, taste, smell, figure, and consistence having been observed to go together, are accounted one distinct thing signified by the name 'apple'; other collections of ideas constitute a stone, a tree, a book, and the like. . . ." [3] But since such "ideas," unlike those of other subscribers to the sense-datum theory, are public, not private, Berkeley calls them "qualities."

In line with the current interest in models, Berkeley's theory of vision is an illustration of the use of a model to make a theory, a procedure resembling Plato's use of the *polis* model in the *Republic*. It illustrates the use of the linguistic model to make the Linguistic Theory of Vision. Corollary to this, it is a work in semantic analysis or synthesis which records discoveries or inventions connected with the relations between words and things and words and actions—discoveries or inventions made again, more recently, by Russell, Wittgenstein, and others. It is such a work on language because models illuminate not only what they model; some of the light they shed is reflected upon themselves: "It may not therefore be amiss to examine the use of other signs in order to know that of words." [4] Thus one might appropriately rename Berkeley's first and last works on vision *An Essay Towards a New Theory*

---

[3] *A Treatise Concerning the Principles of Human Knowledge*, sec. 1, "Library of Liberal Arts," No. 53 (New York, 1957), p. 23.

[4] *Alciphron*, Dial. VII, sec. 5.

of Language and *The Theory of Language or Linguistic Vision,* or *Semantic Analysis* and *Semantic Synthesis,* respectively. Such naming would be consistent with the principle used to name Plato's *Republic,* for this book is called after the model, not after what is modeled.

These are, perhaps, the obvious ways of sorting Berkeley's work. But there are others.

His work is an introduction to the problem of universals, for it asks and tries to answer such questions as: How do particulars become general? and, If common nouns and abstract nouns designate no common natures and no abstract ideas, how do they have meaning?

It is also an argument (as Berkeley intended it to be and Hume [5] apparently thought it was) for the existence of a benevolent, ever-present God whose hypothetical imperatives, if we are not taken in by their ambiguities, prescribe warnings of such future events as precipices, approaching automobiles, and tornadoes.

Moreover, the linguistic model suggests an alternative to the traditional conception of mind according to which the phrase "ideas in the mind" is taken literally, which ideas we introspect and use to make inferences to the external world. For after the great seventeenth-century "discovery" that the eye is a camera that receives *images* of the external world on its screen, it was difficult to resist making a further extension of the application of this appealing model. It was Locke who invented the notion that the whole understanding is a camera that receives the "external visible resemblances or *ideas* of things without." [6]

Berkeley's theory of vision serves also to introduce one side of another important debate—a debate, within the wider nativist-empiricist controversy, between the Berkeleyan and the Kantian theories of our knowledge of space. Indeed, the main

[5] *Dialogues Concerning Natural Religion* (Edinburgh, 1779), Part VI. Some of Cleanthes' ideas represent Berkeley's, and some of the phrases are the same.

[6] *Essay Concerning Human Understanding* (1690), II.xi.17.

issue between Kant and Berkeley reduces to the question of the conception of space. Kant himself was aware of the issue. He knew that Berkeley held that space is "known to us only by means of experience or perception," [7] and he claimed that this view entails the conclusion that "experience is nothing but sheer illusion." [8] Kant also claimed that only his own doctrine, according to which space "inheres in us as a pure form of our sensibility before all perception," [9] avoids illusionism because it affords "the certain criterion for distinguishing truth from illusion." [10]

Finally, it is an introduction to problems in aesthetics. One of these problems is the problem of what the painter actually paints. Berkeley's theory, it was argued by Ruskin, gives the correct solution: "The whole technical power of painting depends on our recovery of what may be called the *innocence of the eye;* that is to say, of a sort of childish perception of these flat stains of color, merely as such, without consciousness of what they signify—as a blind man would see them if suddenly gifted with sight." [11] This idea guided the Impressionists. Another problem is the problem of the interpretation of works of art. Berkeley's theory suggests a solution to this problem. The work of art, whether it be painted, sculptured, or danced, does not hold up a mirror image of its subject but conveys meaning by means of visual language.

4. THE PROBLEM OF VISION

The problem of vision to which Berkeley addressed himself was set by the Greeks. It begins with the consideration of cer-

[7] *Prolegomena to Any Future Metaphysics* (1783), tr. Lewis W. Beck, "Library of Liberal Arts," No. 27 (New York, 1950), p. 124.

[8] *Ibid.*, p. 123.   [9] *Ibid.*, p. 124.

[10] *Ibid.* For a fuller discussion, see my article, "Kant's Refutation of Dogmatic Idealism," *The Philosophical Quarterly*, V, 20 (July, 1955), 225-244.

[11] John Ruskin, *The Elements of Drawing* (London, 1857), note to par. 5, quoted in E. H. Gombrich, *Art and Illusion* (New York, 1960), p. 296.

tain "popular suppositions," [1] the main ones being, strangely enough, that when we see, we are "directly and intuitively" [2] confronted with public three-dimensional physical objects, such as tables, mountains, the sun, the moon, and the remote stars; that in many cases one and the same physical object can be touched, heard, smelled, and tasted, as well as seen; [3] and that these physical objects own properties or have qualities such as their size and shape, which are objects able to be perceived in common by the senses of sight and touch but not by the senses of smell, taste, and hearing.[4]

These suppositions account admirably for ordinary cases of vision. But they run into difficulties in many that are less usual, although not extraordinary. Illusions, hallucinations, the relativity of sense perception, and certain scientific discoveries present problems. The senses, it seems, often deceive us. Macbeth saw a dagger, but could not clutch it. What, then, did he actually see? We see a lake before us in the desert, but we dip our pannikins into sand. We see a yellow cup, but we realize we look with jaundiced eyes. My thumb looks bigger than the Eiffel Tower, but I do not think it is. We see a small round tower in the distance, but we climb a large square building with battlements and turrets. We see a bent stick partly submerged in water, but we pull out a straight one. If we look through a magnifying glass at an object out of focus,

[1] *Visual Language,* sec. 38.

[2] Cf. Samuel Bailey, *A Review of Berkeley's Theory of Vision, designed to show the unsoundness of that celebrated speculation* (London, 1842), pp. 105, 237-38: "We directly and intuitively see objects. . . . This is a simple perception of which no analysis can be given . . . the fact itself cannot be disputed. . . . Metaphysical investigation and physiological inquiry . . . confirm the universal belief of mankind in the direct visual perception of the three dimensions of space."

[3] Cf. Berkeley, *Essay,* sec. 46: " 'Sitting in my study I hear a coach drive along the street; I look through the casement and see it; I walk out and enter into it.' Thus common speech would incline one to think I heard, saw, and touched the same thing, to wit, the coach."

[4] Cf. Berkeley, *Visual Language,* secs. 47, 41: "We suppose an identity of nature, or one and the same thing common to both senses" "such as extension, size, figure, and motion."

as we move the eye backward we notice the object growing nearer and larger, but we know that it is getting farther away. The moon looks bigger at the horizon than at its zenith, but we do not think it really is.

Berkeley himself discussed many of these cases. He used the last two, the Barrovian Case and the Moon Illusion, as test cases for deciding between his linguistic theory and the rival geometrical theory. Cases like these, whether we are genuinely deceived or not, prompted Aristotle and most subsequent scientists to ask such questions as, "How can what we sense be thought identical with the physical object when the latter remains fixed though the former varies?" Their answers persuaded them to give up the popular suppositions of direct realism, though many others have tried valiantly to retain them, and to distinguish what we sense from what we perceive.

Now, although Berkeley never mentioned Aristotle in his writings on vision, it is helpful to consider his account as an attempt to solve the problem set by Aristotle in his *De Anima*. Aristotle's account, however, is ambiguous. My interpretation follows.

What we sense are sense data, the proper objects of each sense. "By a proper object I mean one that cannot be sensed by any other sense and in respect of which no error [or truth] is possible. Thus color is the proper object of sight, sound of hearing, and flavor of taste; while touch, on the other hand, has several proper objects, . . . viz., hot, cold, dry, moist, hard, soft." [5] In receiving these sense data the mind is purely passive, being affected "just as a piece of wax takes on the impress of a signet ring without the iron or gold." [6] The mind is also undeceived, or, rather, neither deceived nor undeceived, for the sense data are "in the mind just as characters may be said

[5] *De Anima* 418a, 423b. This and the following translations of *De Anima* are those of J. A. Smith in *The Works of Aristotle*, ed. W. D. Ross (Oxford, 1931), Vol. III, and *The Basic Works of Aristotle*, ed. R. McKeon (New York, 1941); or those of Philip Wheelwright in *Aristotle* (New York, 1951).

[6] *De Anima* 424a.

to be on a writing tablet on which as yet nothing actually stands written." [7]

What, then, do we perceive? In addition to the proper objects there are objects "common to all the senses," such as size, position, and movement. "There are movements, for example, perceptible to touch as well as sight." [8] But these common objects are not sense data because there is no special sense organ for them. "All of them are *sensed indirectly* as a result of the functioning of the particular senses." [9] There are, moreover, other objects perceived, which Aristotle described merely as "indirectly sensible objects," e.g., "we see that the white object is the son of Diares." [10] If the mind is passive in receiving the sense data, then it is active in perceiving the common and other objects. Therefore, if what we sense are *sense data,* what we perceive are *mind facta.* If the sense data record no lies (and no truths either), then in perceiving we may err. For example, "sight is infallible in its awareness that a certain visual datum is white, although it is perhaps deceived in taking this white datum for a man. . . . For falsehood [and truth] always involve a synthesis." [11] If the sense data are merely characters on Aristotle's writing tablet, then we can infer that the things perceived, the mind facta, are these characters synthesized or composed into sentences. For only sentences can be true or false.

In this fashion Aristotle solved the problem of vision. Seeing is not a simple and direct sensing of physical objects; it is rather a complex conceptual act. It is like making an assertion that something is the case. Some of our assertions are true; others are false. Thus Aristotle solved the problem of visual illusions. There are none. There are only delusions of the active mind. But this solution created a bigger problem. What

---

[7] *De Anima* 430a.   [8] *De Anima* 418a.

[9] *De Anima* 425a. Elsewhere Aristotle speaks as if the common objects are *directly* sensed; e.g., at 418a, but he admits immediately that only the proper objects "are sensed strictly speaking."

[10] *De Anima* 418a.   [11] *De Anima* 430b.

principle enables us to bridge the gap between the sense data and the physical object? Aristotle's answer, "the central sense or general sensibility," [12] left nearly all to be done—but not quite all, because he gave a hint at a most satisfactory solution. The hint he gave was that the sense data are the elements of a language. Two thousand years later, Berkeley took the hint.

5. THE GEOMETRICAL SOLUTION

Among scientists and philosophers from the time of Kepler and Descartes, the most widely held solution to the problem of vision has been the Representative or the Copy or Causal Theory. This solution preserves Aristotle's distinction between what we are directly aware of and what we infer or judge— between sensing and perceiving. In the words of Locke, "the mind knows not things immediately, but by the intervention of ideas it has of them." [1] Because our sense data represent or picture their physical causes, we can make fairly reliable inferences to the external world.

It seems that some such solution is demanded if we take seriously the cases of illusion, hallucination, and relativity, and the great optical, anatomical, and other physical discoveries of the seventeenth century. The Representative Theory was designed to accommodate them. But there have been different versions of this theory. The models used are characteristic of their differences. The main model is found in the Geometrical Theory of Vision.

The history of optics from the Greeks to Kepler records the tortuous search for this model. The success of the search required the formulation of a solution to the mysteries of the function of the eye, including its dioptrics or how the eye forms an image. It is a sorry tale of Western prejudice against

[12] *De Anima* 425a.
[1] *Essay Concerning Human Understanding*, IV.iv.3.

Arab genius, in which, one by one, obstacles were first removed and then restored: the old emission theory, demolished by Ibn al-Haitham but still held by Europeans such as Roger Bacon and Grosseteste; the belief that the crystalline lens, not the retina, was the true photoreceptor, discarded by Ibn Rushd but still held by Europeans; the belief that the retinal image must be erect for erect vision, and so on.

Except for subsequent refinements, the search ended with Kepler's discoveries recorded in his *Supplement to Witelo* (1604) and *Dioptrics* (1611). A century later, these discoveries were presented as Axioms VII and VIII in Newton's *Opticks* (1704).

The model Kepler devised to illustrate how we see had been mentioned by Ibn al-Haitham six hundred years before. "What is true of the camera," Ibn al-Haitham had said, "is true of the eye." The eye is a camera, a machine for taking pictures of the external world. It is equipped with an aperture, a converging lens, a light-sensitive material, a focusing mechanism, and a screen on which pictures of objects, though diminished and inverted, are painted. These pictures or images are now called "real" because the rays of light really meet in them.[2]

Consider how this model illustrates direct vision. Since the eye is an optical system with a converging lens and screen, then, given the distance and size of the object and the focal length of the lens, we can make a graphical construction of the size of the retinal image and, conversely, the distance and size of the object. Kepler provided rules for making these constructions on paper. Then, however, he produced the astonishing rule that, when we see, *we* solve the converse problem just mentioned. Given our own private photograph, we make a deductive inference to the object and locate it at the apex of a triangle from which the rays of light diverge. We use what

[2] Cf. Newton, *Opticks,* Axiom VII, and *Essay,* sec. 88. See also Ibn al-Haitham (Alhazen), *Book of Optics (Opticae Thesaurus Alhazeni Arabis . . .),* tr. from the mid-eleventh-century Arabic by Federico Risnero, (Basle, 1572), Theorem, p. 17, cited in S. L. Polyak, *The Retina* (Chicago, 1941), p. 133. The sentence quoted is my free rendering of Risnero's Latin.

Kepler called the "distance-measuring triangle" [3] to compute the distance and size of the object.

Consider how the model illustrates indirect vision through lenses and mirrors and accounts for the illusions associated with them. Kepler provided another rule. We apply the technique just described, but we ignore the refraction or reflection of the rays, and locate the object at the apex of the triangle from which the rays of light "appear to diverge." [4] The images we see are now called "virtual" because the rays do not meet in them, but only appear to meet. Most mirror and lens illusions are virtual images. For example, we see, through water and air, what seems to be a bent stick, and we see the apparent position of the shark in the aquarium. But only if we make an additional inference do we perceive a straight stick and the true position of the shark.

Thus vision involves, in the words of Descartes, "intricate reasoning similar to that done by geometers." [5] We are able to perform the difficult feat of seeing because we all come into the world equipped with, in the words of Descartes and Leibniz, "a natural geometry." [6] External objects cannot be directly seen. We must, therefore, make inferences to them from the photographs on the back of the camera. These inferences are founded in two different relations. Berkeley described them: We see by inference "founded in a likeness of nature [and] in a geometrical necessity." [7] The inference to the shape, number, and movement of external objects is easy because it is based upon likeness. But we must not infer that external objects are colored. They only appear colored. If, in Newton's words, our retinal images are tinged with yellow, "as in the

[3] "Triangulum distantiae mensorium," from *Supplement to Witelo* (*Ad Vitellionem paralipomena, . . .* [Frankfurt, 1604]), III.ix. Cf. Newton, *Opticks*, Axiom VII; *Essay*, sec. 6.

[4] Cf. Newton, *Opticks*, Axiom VII; *Essay*, secs. 29, 30.

[5] *Dioptrics* (*La dioptrique*, appended to *Discours de la méthode* [Paris, 1637]), VI.13.

[6] *Dioptrics*, VI.13; Leibniz, *New Essays* (*Nouveaux essais sur l'entendement humain* [Amsterdam and Leipzig, 1765]), II.ix.8. Cf. *Essay*, Appendix.

[7] *Visual Language*, sec. 20.

disease of jaundice," then "all objects appear tinged with the same color." [8] Similarly, objects may appear confused or distinct. The inference to the size and distance of external objects is difficult, however, because it involves computation or reckoning from the size of the image. Having demonstrated how we see, Kepler and his followers concluded that when we see, we demonstrate. Leibniz said that we see by "dint of reasoning about rays according to the laws of optics." [9] Berkeley said that the writers on optics think that we see as we deduce "a conclusion in mathematics; betwixt which and the premises it is indeed absolutely requisite there be an apparent necessary connection." [10]

Because of the illumination it seemed to give, the camera model so captured the imagination of scientists and philosophers that they extended its application. Newton applied it only to the eye, but his "under-laborer," Locke, created the popular view of the mind by applying it to the whole understanding:

> For methinks the understanding is not much unlike a closet wholly shut off from light, with only some little openings left, to let in external visible resemblances or ideas of things without. Would the pictures coming into such a dark room but stay there, . . . it would very much resemble the understanding of a man.[11]

The popular idioms—"in the mind" and "image"; "clear," "obscure," "confused" and "distinct" ideas; "introspection" and "reflection"—probably derive from the camera model.

What are its defects? To say that the eye is not really a camera that takes pictures, which we contemplate, is not especially meaningful. We might just as well say that the iron curtain is not really made of iron. Nevertheless, the defects of the camera model outweigh its merits. One defect is that the interpretation of the photograph is not built into the camera. The model is marvelously equipped for taking the picture but

8 *Opticks*, Axiom VII.   9 *New Essays*, II.ix.8.
10 *Essay*, sec. 24.
11 *Essay Concerning Human Understanding*, II.xi.17.

useless in interpreting it. Consider the distinction already made between sense data and mind facta; the camera model nicely illustrates the passive aspect of the mind in vision, but it can shed no light on the active process of perception. It seems to require, behind the camera, a ghost with another pair of eyes who contemplates and interprets the pictures on the camera screen, just as Kepler had to get inside his own camera obscura. In order to meet this difficulty, Descartes merely substituted a different ghost, one who does not *see* the pictures but who *feels* "the movements by which the pictures are formed." [12]

It is interesting to notice the heroic measures adopted to make the camera model work. Embarrassment was caused by the inversion of the picture on the camera screen. How do we see things erect although their images are inverted? One writer, Molyneux, said that the ghost behind the camera "takes no notice of" the inversion although he does notice everything else.[13] Descartes, however, invented an auxiliary model, that of a blind man who "sees with his hands" by holding two crossed sticks, "crossed" in order to reinvert the inversion of the pictures, and "sticks" because the rays of light are straight.[14] Just as this man feels the position of objects without noticing the inverted position of his hands, so does the ghost in the head see the position of objects without noticing the inverted impulse.

A well-known difficulty, also shared by other representative theories, is this: How do we know that our sense data represent physical objects when the latter cannot be experienced? This difficulty prompted philosophers to produce elaborate proofs of the external world. Kepler did not "see" any retinal images except his own. But Descartes thought he did: "Take the eye of a newly dead man. . . . You will see, I dare say with surprise and pleasure, a picture representing in natural per-

---

12 *Dioptrics*, VI.

13 *New Dioptrics* (*Dioptrica nova*, Latin title and English text [London, 1692]), pp. 104-5.

14 *Dioptrics*, VI.

spective all the objects outside." [15] Thus he thought that he could compare the photograph with the original, but he was deluded; according to the theory, he could contemplate only his own images on the back of his own camera and compare them one with another.

Yet another difficulty is that, according to the theory, we make deductive inferences to the external world from our retinal images, but when we see, we do not seem to be aware of the inference or its premise. Accordingly, it was decided that we perform the inference without knowing that we do.

The final difficulty is that the Geometrical Theory really provides no solution to the problem of illusion unless it places a ghost behind the camera screen. But even this is not enough, for the size, shape, and color of the photograph are all that the ghost has to go on. He can make an inference to the crooked oar, but he cannot *see that* it is straight. He can make an inference to the yellow cup, but he cannot *see that* it is white. He cannot solve the problem of the horizontal moon because the size of its image hardly varies. In many cases where we see images through lenses and mirrors, the ghost should not see anything at all because there is no virtual image. He cannot tell which is bigger, his thumb, or the Eiffel Tower, because at some times the visual thumb is much bigger, at others, the visual tower. He must even be fooled by the images seen in the plane mirror. In all these cases he must be fooled by the *ambiguities* of vision in much the same way as children are fooled by metaphors. He must be fooled unless he is a ghost who can *interpret* what he sees from the *information* given to him, a ghost with a memory who can tell what things *signify,* and who, aware of *contexts,* can see through the *ambiguities* and *double talk* of vision. In short, he must be fooled unless he has learned to *understand* the "words" of the language of vision.

[15] *Ibid.*

6. THE LINGUISTIC SOLUTION

Berkeley demonstrated how it is possible to talk in this way about vision. By representing the facts in idioms appropriate to language, he was able to suggest satisfactory solutions to various problems of vision. Others before him—Plato, Aristotle, Glanvill, Cudworth, Descartes, Locke—had used some features of language to illustrate vision or perception, but none had used as many, and none had used them to make a whole theory. In the following paragraphs, I shall exhibit some of the features of Berkeley's linguistic model and suggest how he used them to illuminate the problems of vision. Clearly he had in mind an ordinary language like English, already in existence, and, more often, a spoken rather than a written language.

(1) Language is "the arbitrary use of sensible signs" invented for purposes not only of *communication* but of *rousing emotion* and *directing action*.[1]

To see is largely "to foresee"[2] so that we may take action. The signs must be sensible: "When I perceive your meaning by your words, must I not first perceive the words themselves?"[3] The words of an ordinary or of visual language function as *signs of* things or as *signs for* action or as *cues for* passion. When uttered or presented they may make us think of physical objects absent or distant from our bodies, or they may make us leap straight into action or passion "without any ideas coming between."[4]

How does Berkeley interpret the signs and the things they signify in order to make his theory true? Although he is aware "how hard it is for anyone to hear [or see] the words of his native language . . . without understanding them" and how

1 *Alciphron*, Dial. IV, sec. 7.
2 *Essay*, sec. 59.
3 *Alciphron*, Dial. IV, sec. 8. Cf. *Essay*, secs. 9, 10.
4 *Principles*, Introduction, sec. 20.

hard it is "to disunite the meaning" [5] from the sounds or colors, he realizes that much can be said about the latter. Berkeley specifies the properties of visual objects. They are colors; they have, *so to speak,* size, shape, situation, and motion, and they are faint or clear, confused or distinct. Thus, for example, in my visual field my thumb is a shade bigger than the Eiffel Tower; it is higher than the tower, and is distinct while the latter is confused. Nevertheless, visual objects lack the dimension of depth or distance among themselves; like the words on this page, or like rainbows, colors have no backs to them. They also lack depth in relation to what they signify. Certainly it would be strange to expect words to be near to or far from what they are used to mean. Berkeley specifies that "the proper objects of sight are at no distance, neither near nor far from any tangible thing." [6] Finally, therefore, they lack depth in relation to the eye of the interpreter, which eye is felt, not seen. Accordingly, if visual objects are not solid, neither are they flat or plane (which means that "they appear to the touch smooth and uniform")[7] "since some idea of distance is necessary to form the idea of a geometrical plane." [8]

By specifying these features it is clear that Berkeley intends that visual objects are not in space. They are merely a "set of thoughts or sensations" [9] that exist only in the mind, and spatial terms, such as "large" or "small," "high" or "low," "fast" or "slow," are not to be applied to these thoughts "except only in a metaphorical sense." [10] It is otherwise with the things signified. These he interprets as physical objects that exist "without his mind in the ambient space." [11] In a literal sense they are plane or solid objects at a distance; they have size, shape, and situation; and they are in motion or at rest. Berkeley identifies these physical objects with tactual objects

5 *Essay,* sec. 159.   6 *Essay,* sec. 112.
7 *Essay,* sec. 157.   8 *Essay,* sec. 155.
9 *Essay,* sec. 41.
10 *Essay,* sec. 94. See below, rule 9, p. xxxv.
11 *Ibid.*

because he assumes that the congenitally blind may know all about space and the objects in it.[12]

Berkeley now addresses himself to the most vexing problem of language. What is the connection between the signs and the things signified? But first, what is it not? In the next three features Berkeley deprives himself of any recourse to the picture theory of language, the theory that the structure or the elements of our language actually mirror the structure or the elements of the world.

(2) The signs of a language are not pictures of or necessarily connected with the things signified.[13]

For example, the size, shape, and situation of the combination, "This is a dagger," do not copy or re-present the size, shape, and situation of the state of affairs that this sentence so readily suggests to us, nor can we deduce the latter from the former. The two things are "specifically distinct" or "heterogeneous." So is it with visual signs and the things they signify. "This main part and pillar" [14] of Berkeley's theory of language is true, so he argues, because—

(3) If the signs were pictures, etc., then we could interpret them although they had not been ostensively defined for us; [15] and—

(4) The consequent of (3) is false; that is, we cannot interpret them unless they have been ostensively defined for us.[16]

"To interpret a thing" means "to tell what it signifies." [17]

[12] Cf. M. von Senden, *Space and Sight* (Glencoe, Ill.: The Free Press, 1960; tr. Peter Heath, from German edn., 1932), p. 309. Von Senden disagrees: "We have been led to conclude that by tactual perception alone the patient is unable to acquire an awareness of space, and that this is solely dependent on visual perception."

[13] Cf. *Visual Language*, secs. 41, 42, 20; *Essay*, secs. 127, 128.

[14] *Visual Language*, sec. 41.

[15] Cf. *Essay*, sec. 133; *Visual Language*, sec. 44.

[16] *Ibid.* Cf. also *Alciphron*, Dial. IV, sec. 11. Since Berkeley wants to hold that we see such things as the moon and the planets, rules 3 and 4 should demand that only our *basic* vocabulary is learned ostensively.

[17] *Siris*, sec. 253.

An ostensive definition consists in "the establishment of an association through the hearing [or seeing, etc.] of closely similar sounds [or colors, etc.] whenever the object to be defined is present." [18] If we are to tell what something signifies, then "there must be time and experience, by repeated acts, to acquire a habit of knowing the connection." [19]

How does Berkeley test this part of his theory? He deduces that a foreigner to a language cannot at first understand it. "A Chinese," for example, "upon first hearing the words 'man' and 'tree,' would not think of the things signified by them." [20] Similarly, he deduces his answer to the famous problem of Molyneux.[21] Since vision is a language, it follows that a foreigner to visual language cannot at first understand it. For example, "a man born blind and made to see [upon first 'seeing' colors] would never think of men, trees, or any other objects

[18] Bertrand Russell, *Human Knowledge* (New York, 1948), p. 501.

[19] *Alciphron*, Dial. IV, sec. 11.

[20] *Ibid.*

[21] Cf. *Essay*, secs. 132-5. Molyneux sent the problem to his friend Locke in 1693. Locke published it in the *Essay Concerning Human Understanding* (2nd edn., 1694), II.ix.8. The problem is: Can a man born blind and made to see distinguish a globe from a cube by sight before he touches them? The problem became a central one in eighteenth-century epistemology and psychology. Ernst Cassirer says: "A survey of the special problems of eighteenth-century epistemology and psychology shows that in all their variety and inner diversity they are grouped around a common center. The investigation of individual problems in all their abundance and apparent dispersion comes back again and again to a general theoretical problem [the problem of Molyneux] in which all the threads of the study unite." (*The Philosophy of the Enlightenment* [Princeton, 1951], p. 108.) M. von Senden says that his book "took its starting point from the celebrated problem of Molyneux." (*Space and Sight*, p. 309. See also p. 17.) The problem focuses upon the issue between nativists or rationalists and empiricists. The former answer Molyneux's question affirmatively because they hold that there is an inner connection or common nature between the fields of sight and touch (cf. rule 3) enabling us, for example, to see the same round shape that we feel. The latter, because they give a negative answer (cf. rule 4) conclude that there is no common nature (cf. rule 2). See also rules 8, 9, 10, below and my note to *Essay*, sec. 132.

that he had been accustomed to perceive by touch." [22] He would prove quite unable to recognize what they are or to name them. He would get no meaning from the mass of colors before his eyes. That is, he would not be able to see.[23]

Having divorced himself from all picture theories of language, Berkeley has not yet answered the main problem: How are the words of vision connected with their referents? In the

[22] *Alciphron*, Dial. IV, sec. 11.

[23] But can Berkeley's hypothesis, the "main part and pillar" of his theory of vision, that is, rule 2 interpreted, be confirmed or disconfirmed? Now when Berkeley wrote the *Essay*, no experimental reports of cases of people born blind and made to see were available to him. In the Appendix to the second edition (see Appendix to *Essay*, p. 101), he referred to a case only briefly. But by the time he wrote *Visual Language*, the report on the Cheselden case (see *Visual Language*, sec. 71) was available to him. Berkeley said that the experiment confirmed some "points" of his theory. Several cases have been reported since the famous Cheselden case. Here are portions of three typical reports, quoted by von Senden in *Space and Sight:*

1. *Raehlmann's Case* (1891): "He is shown a sphere and a cube, both of the same colored wood and of similar cross-section. On looking at them together he realizes that the two are distinct, but *does not know which* is round and which cornered" (p. 114; italics mine).

2. *Nunneley's Case* (before 1855): "He could at once perceive a difference in their shapes; though he *could not in the least say which* was the cube and which the sphere, he saw they were not of the same figure" (p. 106; italics mine).

3. *Dufour's Case* (1875): " 'Do you know what a square is?'—He positions his two hands so that they form a pair of surfaces which make contact almost at right angles along the radial edge. He thereby produces an angle, which is actually part of a cube. 'And a circle?'—He again bends his hand round with the fingers pointing towards the wrist, and thereby produces an almost complete ring. After this fashion he therefore has some knowledge of circularity. In looking at the watch, at which his gaze is obviously directed, he remains *absolutely incapable of saying whether* it is round or cornered. However much I insist on an answer, none is forthcoming. . . . On the following morning the same question; the same inability to answer. So I then let him feel the watch. No sooner has he taken it in his hand than he immediately says, 'That's round, it's a watch' " (p. 108; italics mine).

next three features, Berkeley suggests the solution to the problem set by Aristotle—

(5) The converse of (4) is true: Language is learned by the
"constant and long association of ideas entirely different," [24]
that is, by ostensive definition.

After the sounds or colors are ostensively defined by "repeated acts," a foreigner to the language will "consider them
as signs," [25] and will be able to tell what they signify. The
process is arduous and irksome, the achievement difficult in
languages either verbal or visual. It takes months, or even
years, for a foreigner to learn to interpret noises or colors. This
requires that the foreigner has a memory enabling him to
make inductive leaps. Accordingly—

(6) Our expectations or "prenotions concerning the kind,
size, shape, and nature of things" condition the meanings we
give to the words we see or hear.[26]

Interpretation, whether in reading a page, listening to a
lecture, or seeing a landscape, is conditioned by what we expect.[27] To a marked extent we see what we are looking for
because we are thinking of it. Man Friday looked and saw
nothing, but Crusoe looked and *saw that* it was a ship. Macbeth saw a dagger, and Hamlet the ghost of his father.

Nevertheless, we often misinterpret our cues. However, both
the sources of our error and the means for its avoidance are
conveniently specified in the linguistic model. First, the
sources—

(7-a) Words are often ambiguous, that is, they do not "always suggest things in the same uniform way and have the
same constant regular connection with matters of fact." [28]

---

24 *Philosophical Commentaries*, Entry 225. Cf. *Essay*, secs. 25, 62; *Visual
Language*, sec. 47. Once more, Berkeley might have said that only our
basic visual vocabulary need be learned ostensively.

25 *Visual Language*, sec. 45.

26 *Visual Language*, sec. 59.

27 Cf. E. H. Gombrich, *Art and Illusion*, p. 303.

28 *Alciphron*, Dial. IV, sec. 12.

Without the means whereby we may avoid being taken in by the ambiguities of visual language called, in ordinary language, "visual illusions," "we should no more have taken blushing for a sign of shame than of gladness," [29] or a bent appearance for a sign of a straight stick than of a crooked one.

(7-b) Many words are meaningful although they denote nothing.[30] For example, "we may sometimes perceive colors where there is nothing to be felt." [31] Without the means whereby we may avoid being fooled by these non-denoting symbols called, in ordinary language "mirages," and "hallucinations," the pragmatic value of vision would cease. What, then, is the means whereby we may avoid error?

(7-c) The context of the word provides the means whereby we may avoid error, for "a word pronounced with certain circumstances or in a certain context with other words has not always the same import and signification that it has when pronounced in some other circumstances or different context of words." [32]

In order to solve the problems created by the frequently encountered cases of ambiguity and absence of designation of the words of visual language, Berkeley leans heavily upon his context theory of meaning. Only after long experience of different contexts and the remembrance of them are we able to avoid being victimized by the metaphors, other ambiguities, and non-denoting symbols of visual language, so that we can *see that* such things as sticks, crooked in the context of water and air, are really straight, that the blush that suffuses a cheek means gladness and not shame, and that the object appearing before our eyes as a dagger is to be correctly *interpreted* as "a dagger of the mind" and not a real one. *We* are able, and so it is amusing to watch monkeys being fooled by the ambiguous language of the plane mirror. In these examples we cannot say that the appearances of the stick, the blush, and the dagger are either erroneous or true. We might just as well say that the words "stick," "blush," and "dagger" are true or false. But we

29 *Essay*, sec. 65.
31 *Essay*, sec. 103.
30 Cf. *Essay*, sec. 64.
32 *Essay*, sec. 73.

can say that the sentence, "This is a dagger of the mind," is true or false.

Berkeley has not yet solved the problem of vision. He has shown that visual data are signs of physical objects, but people commonly say and believe otherwise. They say and believe that the cup they see is the same thing as the physical cup. Accordingly, Berkeley tries to accommodate common-sense notions. With great ingenuity he specifies three additional features in the linguistic model:

(8-a) We sometimes want to talk *about* a language as well as *from within* it. When this is done it is customary to call the signs by "the same names with the things signified." [33] This custom is highly convenient. If we were not to adopt it, "the endless number or confusion of names would render language impracticable." [34] Thus when we use a spoken language, "it is customary to *call* written words and the things they signify by the same name." [35] We use, for example, the phonetic sequence ɪŋglɪʃ to name both the written and the spoken languages, the phonemes ɛɣ to name the character "a" and its corresponding sounds, and the sounds skwɛːʀ to name both the figure square and the six characters used to mark it. Similarly, in the written language of music, a mark on a page is used to name a sound. But in the spoken language of English both the mark and the sound are called by such same names as **nowt** and **haɣ** or **low**. Similarly, in the traditional language of painting, whose words (like those of the Author of Nature himself) are color combinations, a certain combination is used to signify a situation. But in English language both are called by such names as those written "landscape," "view," or "still life."

Similarly, in the language of vision a certain combination of colors signifies a certain large, high, square tower a long way off. In English, however, both this sign and the thing it signi-

[33] *Visual Language*, sec. 45.
[34] *Three Dialogues Between Hylas and Philonous*, "Library of Liberal Arts," No. 39 (New York, 1954), Dial. III, p. 93.
[35] *Essay*, sec. 140.

fies are called by the same names as those written "large,"
"high," "square," and "far"—the same names as those used by
a blind Englishman who has walked to and explored the
tower. But why does the thing signified confer its name on the
sign rather than the converse?

(8-b) "Signs being little considered in themselves or for their
own sake, . . . the mind often overlooks them, so as to carry
its attention immediately on to the things signified," where
nearly all our interest lies.[36] Our interest lies more in tactual
objects because sticks and stones may break our bones, but
names will never hurt us.[37] Hence Pavlov's dog was more interested in his food than in the sound of the bell, while we are
generally more interested in the feel of precipices and port-
manteaux than in their looks.

(9) But these common names do not name common natures
or abstract ideas.

What, then, is the nature of such shared naming? "This proceeds only from experience and analogy. There is a *higher*
and *lower* in the notes of music. Men speak in a high or a
low key. And this, it is plain, is no more than metaphor or
analogy." [38] Thus when we speak of such things as high notes,
cold shoulders, and bitter words, we speak in metaphor. Berkeley is merely applying the traditional or Aristotelian definition
of metaphor: "Metaphor consists in giving the thing a name
that belongs to something else," where the transference may,
but need not, be based upon resemblance.[39] Thus when an
original "sort-crosser" decides that a mark on a musical score
and a sound are to have the name "high" in common, he need
find no common nature or abstract idea *height*, or, indeed, any

---

[36] *Alciphron*, Dial. VII, sec. 12. Cf. Locke, *Essay*, II.ix.9: "A man who
reads or hears with attention and understanding . . . takes little notice
of the characters or sounds but of the ideas that are excited in him by
them." Cf. also Descartes, *The World* (*Le monde* [Paris, 1664]), chap. 1:
We understand what words signify "even without our paying attention to
the sound of the words or to their syllables."

[37] Cf. *Essay*, sec. 59.   [38] *Visual Language*, sec. 46.

[39] *Poetics* 1457b.

resemblance between the height of a mark on a page and the "height" of a sound, though his decision may create the illusion of resemblance.

But to the astonishment of posterity Berkeley lets the argument lead: "So likewise to express the order of visible ideas, the words 'situation,' 'high' and 'low,' 'up' and 'down,' are made use of, and their sense when so applied is analogical." [40] Obviously this applies not only to situation words but to distance words, size words, and motion words, if they are used to express the order of visual objects.

(10) But if the language is learned in our "earliest infancy," that is, if the connection between the signs and the things signified is "sucked in with our milk" so that we cannot remember having learned the correlation; if the language is the same all over the world; and if in our native tongue we call its signs and the things signified by the same names, then we are prone to "confound in this language of vision the signs with the things signified," and "we suppose an identity of nature." The signs and their referents are "complicated," "twisted," "knotted," or "concreted" together.[41]

What were merely common names are now supposed to name common natures. It is easy to conceive how this occurs. Consider that the same consequence often ensues with languages that are neither universal nor learned in earliest infancy. Berkeley calls this "popular supposition" a prejudice, "which prejudice," he says, "suits well enough with the purposes of life, and language is suited to this prejudice." [42]

Using these rules of grammar and supplementing them according to his need, Berkeley explains how we tell by sight the situation, size, and distance of physical objects. The problem he solves is much like the problem, "Given such words as 'big' and 'small,' 'high' and 'low,' 'near' and 'far,' how do we *tell*

---

[40] *Visual Language,* sec. 46.
[41] *Visual Language,* sec. 47; *Alciphron,* Dial. VII, sec. 11; *Essay,* sec. 144.
[42] *Visual Language,* sec. 35.

what they mean?" Thus vision is a public and objective affair. Since the words of visual language are "fixed and immutably the same in all times and places," [43] and since we do the *telling* in another public language, namely, our own native but artificial tongue, we can communicate what we see. But vision is also a private and subjective affair. Owing to our prenotions and prejudices, which are conditioned by all that we have met, and owing to the fact that the words of our own language are "variable and uncertain, depending altogether on the arbitrary appointment of men," [44] it is unlikely that different people will give exactly the same meanings to the words of visual language.

7. TEST CASES

In order to test his theory against the rival Geometrical Theory, Berkeley tries to solve three celebrated cases of visual illusion, one each for how we manage to tell or mistell by sight the situation, the size, and the distance of material things. By the rival theory these problems are either insoluble or soluble only extravagantly. In illusion, as its name implies, we are played against or mocked, and often cheated or deceived. Berkeley asks: "What is it can put this cheat on the understanding?" [1] Such cheats generate the problem of vision and, indeed, the whole problem of perception. Without them the problem might never have been posed. In every case Berkeley accepts the facts discovered by the scientists, though some of them beg for clarification. Then he asks what principles can best accommodate the apparently contrary facts. Thus, granted that our retinal images are *inverted*, "how comes it to pass that the objects whereof the pictures are thus inverted do yet *seem erect?*" [2] Granted that the visual angle (measured with a goniometer) under which we see the horizontal moon is *smaller* than it is for the meridional moon,

---

[43] *Essay*, sec. 152.
[1] *Essay*, sec. 74.

[44] *Ibid.*
[2] *Visual Language*, sec. 49 (italics mine).

"how comes it, therefore, to *seem greater* in one situation than in another?" [3] Granted that, as we draw the eye backward, the object placed beyond the focus of a magnifying glass or concave mirror is getting *farther away*, why does it *seem to draw nearer?*

In trying to solve the first of these problems, subscribers to the Geometrical Theory had to resort to heroic measures.[4] They could find no geometrical solution to the second problem and were forced to resort to psychological solutions.[5] To the third problem also no geometrical solution was forthcoming. The image seen in this, the Barrovian Case, is indeed inexplicable on the principles of geometrical optics, for it is neither *real* (the rays do not actually pass through it) nor *virtual* (the rays cannot be projected to pass through it). This image or effigy, therefore, should not exist. Yet Barrow and Tacquet saw it, and anyone can confirm its existence. Berkeley claims that this case "entirely subverts" the received theories.[6] Reviewing these solutions, Berkeley concludes that the laws of geometrical optics, considered as an explanation of how we see, "will not stand." [7]

His own solutions to these problems are, I believe, applications of the rules I have given in section 6 above, basically rules 2 and 5. Throughout his account, however, he often applies features of the language model without saying so.

This is true especially of his solution of the "knot" about inverted images. Berkeley calls his solution "the principal point in the whole optic theory." [8] It is the principal point be-

---

[3] *Essay,* sec. 74. (italics mine).

[4] See above, sec. 5; *Essay,* secs. 89, 90.

[5] *Essay,* secs. 75, 76.

[6] *Essay,* sec. 33. This problem, like that of the Moon Illusion, remains very much alive. See Ronchi, *Optics: The Science of Vision,* chap. 4, especially secs. 138-41, 169-70, 190-96. See also my articles, "Berkeley and Ronchi on Optics," *Proceedings XII International Congress of Philosophy,* XII (1961), 453-60; "Grosseteste and an Ancient Optical Principle," *Isis,* L, 162 (December, 1959), 467-72. See also *Essay,* sec. 29, notes 27, 29.

[7] *Visual Language,* sec. 32.

[8] *Visual Language,* sec. 52. See my article, "Berkeley and Molyneux on

cause it exhibits the fullest application of the "main part and pillar" of his theory.[9] That is to say, it is an application of his principal theorem, namely, the heterogeneity of the words and referents of visual language (rule 2).[10] How easily is the problem solved once we utilize the "machinery" of language, partially hidden in Berkeley's account! For it takes only a few days to adapt to the words of an ordinary or of visual language if its words are written upside down. Neither would the marks ɪɴᴠᴇʀᴛᴇᴅ come to mean "erect" nor would the visual Eiffel Tower come to mean the Eiffel Well.[11]

Berkeley's solution of the famous puzzle known as the "Moon Illusion"[12] manifests the application of various features of the linguistic model. Here is a problem whose solution demands ingredients which, when put together, seem to be uniquely the properties of language. It seems that in order to solve it we must make a distinction similar to that made between words and their referents—we tend to overlook the words, the meaning we give is largely subjective, to some peo-

---

Retinal Images," *Journal of the History of Ideas*, XVI, 3 (June, 1955), 339-55.

9 *Visual Language*, sec. 41.

10 In his solution Berkeley states the theorem and then adds: "But more especially throughout the consideration of this affair, we ought to carry that distinction in our thoughts" (*Essay*, sec. 91).

11 The results of this experiment, suggested by Berkeley in *Philosophical Commentaries*, Entry 278, and since performed by a few experimenters of whom G. M. Stratton was probably the first, confirm Berkeley's solution to the problem of inversion. (See G. M. Stratton, "Vision Without Inversion of the Retinal Image," *Psychological Review*, IV, 5 [September, 1897], 341-60, 463-81.) Berkeley's solution also provided him with an important link between his theory of vision and his metaphysics. See my article, "The Influence of Berkeley's Science on His Metaphysics," *Philosophy and Phenomenological Research*, XVI, 4 (June, 1956), 476-87.

12 This problem has a long history. It has puzzled some of the best thinkers from Ptolemy through Bacon, Hobbes, Descartes, Helmholtz, and a host of others, to the present. See H. Leibowitz and T. Hartman, "Magnitude of the Moon Illusion as a Function of the Age of the Observer," *Science*, CXXX, 4 (September, 1959), 569-70; L. Kaufman and I. Rock, "The Moon Illusion," *Scientific American*, CCVII, 1 (July, 1962), 120-28.

ple the two moons look equally big, and the meaning is relative to time and place. But most characteristic of Berkeley's solution is the use he makes of the Context Principle of Meaning (rule 7-c above).[13]

His solution of the Barrovian Case [14] is ingenious. If we are not cheated by this "certain odd and particular" [15] illusion, as usually we are not, then, as we draw the eye backward, we *see that* the object placed beyond the focus of a magnifying glass is receding from us. But why does it *seem* to draw nearer? Barrow wanted a solution that would exclude "all prenotions and prejudices." [16] The object is a point source and factors such as visual size are not to count. Barrow argued that the object ought to appear to be extremely remote because diverging rays mean near, parallel rays mean far, therefore converging rays mean very far. But when he looked he found that the facts were directly opposite, that is, the object appeared to be extremely near. Nonplussed, he refused to renounce his theory according to which "every object appears by so much the farther off by how much the rays it sends to the eye are less diverging," [17] and he concluded that in this case "something peculiar lies hidden" that neither he nor anyone before him had been able to discover.

With the help of his language model Berkeley was able to reveal the peculiar nature of what lay hidden and thereby to offer a plausible explanation of this strange phenomenon. Since it is a case of illusion, it is appropriately treated as a case of ambiguity in the words of visual language (see rule 7). Accordingly, there should be one sign that has two meanings, the one apparent and mistaken, the other real and hidden. But here is an *odd and particular case* of ambiguity because one meaning is the direct opposite of the other.[18] Why, then, does something seem to be signified when in fact its exact contrary is signified? Why, in other words, does the object seem

---

[13] *Essay*, sec. 73.

[14] See note 6 above and *Essay*, sec. 29.

[15] *Essay*, sec. 29.   [16] *Ibid.*

[17] *Ibid.*   [18] *Essay*, sec. 32.

to draw near when in fact it recedes? It is because there is present here a sign that unavoidably suggests near distance, that is, a feature customarily associated with it in vision. What is it? Berkeley isolates visual confusion or fuzziness as the feature common to the two situations.[19]

What experiment would test Berkeley's solution? Since he knows that an ambiguous expression preserves its identity throughout the diversity of its meaning, Berkeley is able to devise an experiment [20] in which a person with normal eyesight is made to experience visual confusion in two different ways: He is made to receive first diverging rays that meet behind the retina and then converging rays that meet before the retina (the Barrovian Case) so as to produce similar circles of confusion on the retina; and Berkeley predicts that the subject of the experiment will be unable to tell the difference.[21] If Berkeley is right he may have solved the abstract problem as it was posed by Barrow. In concrete cases, which we often encounter now that lenses are so common, the increasing visual size concurs with the increasing confusion to magnify the illusion, for the visual size increases as the apparent distance of the object decreases, that is, as the real distance increases.[22]

How, then, do we avoid being cheated? This is like asking how we avoid being taken in by the ambiguities of ordinary language. We do so by making use of our prenotions and contextual factors that are neutralized in Barrow's presentation of the problem.

8. THE NEW THEORY AND IMMATERIALISM

Clearly, Berkeley thought that his theory of vision could be made to support his immaterialism, for after publishing the

---

[19] *Essay*, sec. 31.   [20] *Essay*, secs. 35, 36.

[21] Berkeley's contention is questioned in M. H. Pirenne's "Physiological Mechanisms in the Perception of Distance by Sight and Berkeley's Theory of Vision," *British Journal for the Philosophy of Science*, IV, 13 (May, 1953), 13-21.

[22] *Visual Language*, secs. 64, 68.

Essay he wrote to Percival: "I hope to make what is there laid down appear subservient to the ends of morality and religion in a treatise [the *Principles*] I have now in the press." [1]

How are the two theories connected?

Berkeley's ulterior design was to destroy skepticism and atheism; his method was to destroy their foundations. Nearest the ground lay materialism.[2] This doctrine was traditionally described in a mixed vocabulary probably derived from the language of subjects, predicates, and cameras: There are two sorts of subject, thing, or substance in the world, one mental, the other material. The predicates, qualities, or attributes of mental substance are ideas; those of material substance are primary qualities. Some of our ideas of material things are pictures, while all are effects, of the primary qualities of material things which exist outside the mind; the latter must be known by inference from our pictures. This doctrine, Berkeley argues, leads to skepticism because we can never check our pictures against their originals, and to atheism because these originals, elbowing God out of his traditional causal role, make him redundant.

Paradoxically, in the *Essay* Berkeley makes no frontal assault upon materialism. Instead he prepares it for ultimate demolition by undermining it, by means of the application of the language model to vision with the camera model as its auxiliary.

First, he interprets the referents of the words of visual language as material things and, although he allows them to

---

[1] March 1, 1710, in *The Works of George Berkeley, Bishop of Cloyne*, ed. A. A. Luce and T. E. Jessop (Edinburgh, 1948-1957), VIII, 31.

[2] This is grounded in the doctrine of abstract ideas and in category-mistakes. These, in turn, are ultimately based upon the abuses of proper names and metaphors. For a brief account of the whole architectonic, see my article, "Berkeley's Two Concepts of Mind," *Philosophy and Phenomenological Research*, XX, 1 (September, 1959), 85-92; and my introduction to Berkeley, *A Treatise Concerning the Principles of Human Knowledge*, "Library of Liberal Arts," No. 53 (New York, 1957), pp. xiii-xvii.

"exist without the mind in the ambient space," [3] he construes them as tactual objects. Thus matter can be touched (rule 1).

Secondly, he keeps the pictures in the camera; that is, in terms of the thing modeled, he allows that visual ideas exist only in the mind. But he drops their functions as pictures and effects of matter. Instead he makes them function as words, and words need not be icons or effects of what they mean (rules 2-4). They are connected with their referents or otherwise acquire meaning through ostensive definitions and their use in different contexts (rules 5-7). In order to do this, however, he must first relinquish a linguistic position just as strongly entrenched as materialism, namely, the picture theory of language. This done, Berkeley might have described his extraordinary achievement: "I began by dropping the picture theory of language and ended by adopting the language theory of pictures." [4] Thus the sapper's job on "the received theories, which are as much ruined as mine is established, by this main part and pillar thereof" [5] is almost as good as done.

Thirdly, he shows how visual ideas and tactual objects are complicated or interwoven so that, although they get common names such as "large," "high," and "square," these common names name no common natures, including the common thing or substance of materialism (rules 8-9): " 'Sitting in my study I hear a coach drive along the street; I look through the casement and see it; I walk out and enter into it.' Thus common speech would incline one to think I heard, saw, and touched the same thing, to wit, the coach." [6] This anticipates full immaterialism. For according to materialists the word "coach" denotes a subject, or substance distinct from its qualities which are predicated of it, and in which they exist.[7] To immaterialists, on the other hand, to say that a coach is four-wheeled,

---

3 *Essay,* sec. 94.

4 Nelson Goodman, "The Way the World Is," *Review of Metaphysics,* XIV, 1 (September, 1960), 55, 56.

5 *Visual Language,* sec. 41.   6 *Essay,* sec. 46.

7 Cf. *Principles,* sec. 49.

etc., is to give only an explication of the meaning of the word "coach." [8] Berkeley thus drops the subject-predicate model and adopts that of definiens-definiendum. For example, certain linguistic combinations in the universal language of nature, conventionally called in the particular language of English "four-wheeled," etc., are also conventionally called "coach." Or, in terms of the discarded model, the coach is "nothing distinct from" its qualities. But qualities, in turn, are not things distinct from ideas because Berkeley no longer needs this distinction; moreover, he can find no difference.[9] They exist in the subject mind not as qualities of it but as ideas in it. In the *Essay* the sign relation holds only between visual ideas and tactual objects and is asymmetrical. But in full immaterialism this relation is symmetrical and its terms are extended to include gustatory, auditory, and olfactory ideas— visual guesses being confirmable or disconfirmable by tastes, sounds, and smells, as well as by feels. The same applies to tactual, gustatory, auditory, and olfactory guesses. For example, I smell an onion; that is, I tell that it is an onion by smelling, and I confirm or disconfirm that it is by looking and tasting. "I tell" because I say to myself, "This is an onion"; that is, "This combination of smells, tastes, and looks deserves to be called, in English, 'onion.'"

Accordingly, as far as the *Essay* is concerned matter still exists. But its character is remade. No longer is it beyond the reach of experience; no longer do we see pictures of it or the effects of it; no longer is it a subject or substance that supports attributes. In the *Principles,* tactual objects are explicitly on the same footing as the objects of the other senses and their previous nominal existence without the mind is referred to as "that vulgar error." [10]

Now that matter can be experienced, skepticism is avoidable. No longer are all of us the constant victims of one giant

[8] *Ibid.*

[9] *Principles,* sec. 5, especially the first edition; see Library of Liberal Arts edition, p. 25, note 2.

[10] *Principles,* sec. 44.

illusion. Surely, Berkeley thinks, whenever we are in doubt we can check our pictures against their originals, or, more appropriately, we can "cash" the signs in the things they signify to us. Now that matter ceases to be an agent, the chief ground of atheism is removed. God no longer has a rival for his causal role. Berkeley's analogical argument for the existence of God is exactly the same as his analogical argument for the existence of another person, and "nothing so much convinces me of the existence of another person as his speaking to me." [11] It is once more, therefore, an application of his language model. He who upholds "all things by the word of his power" [12] is alone the Author of the language of nature. But whether Berkeley is a fundamentalist in these matters or whether, finding the old arguments outmoded, he is now offering a modern parable are questions that I leave with the reader to pursue and apply in his own thoughts.

COLIN MURRAY TURBAYNE

[11] *Alciphron,* Dial. IV, sec. 6.
[12] *Principles,* sec. 141.

CHRONOLOGY

1685   George Berkeley born at Kilkenny, March 12
1696   Entered Kilkenny College
1700   Entered Trinity College, Dublin
1704   Received baccalaureate degree
1707   Junior Fellow; M.A.
1709   Ordained deacon; Librarian
1710   Ordained priest; Junior Dean
1712   Junior Greek Lecturer
1713   To London; went to Italy, October
1714   Returned to England
1721   To Dublin; took degrees of B.D. and D.D.; appointed Divinity Lecturer
1722   Appointed Senior Proctor; presented by the Crown to the deanery of Dromore, but the Crown's right to appoint challenged by the Bishop; to London
1723   Returned to Dublin; appointed Hebrew Lecturer; executor and legatee of Hester Van Homrigh
1724   Resigned from Trinity College to become Dean of Derry; to London to raise funds for Bermuda project and get Royal Charter
1726   House of Commons voted a grant for St. Paul's College, Bermuda
1728   Married Anne Forster; sailed for America
1729   Arrived Newport
1731   Left for England
1732   Nominated Dean of Down, but not appointed
1734   Bishop of Cloyne
1741   Declined offer of nomination for Vice-Chancellorship of Dublin University
1745   Declined offer of Bishopric of Clogher
1752   To Oxford
1753   Died, January 14; interred in the Chapel of Christ Church, Oxford

SELECTED BIBLIOGRAPHY [1]

1. EDITIONS OF BERKELEY'S WORKS

An Essay Towards a New Theory of Vision

EDITIONS PUBLISHED BY BERKELEY

Dublin, 1709.

Dublin, 1710.

Annexed to first edition of *Alciphron*. Dublin and London, 1732.

Annexed to second edition of *Alciphron*. London, 1732.

POSTHUMOUS OR OTHER EDITIONS

With introduction to *A Treatise Concerning the Principles of Human Knowledge*, Italian translation. Venice, 1732.

Annexed to *Alciphron*, French translation by B. DE JONCOURT. Paris, 1734.

In *Works*, 2 vols., edited probably JOSEPH STOCK. Dublin and London, 1784 (reprinted 1820 and 1837).

In *Works*, 2 vols., edited G. N. WRIGHT. London, 1843.

In *Works*, 4 vols., edited A. C. FRASER. Oxford, 1871.

In *Oeuvres Choisies*, French translation by G. BEAULAVON and D. PARODI. Paris, 1895.

In *Works*, 3 vols., edited G. SAMPSON. London, 1897-8.

In *Works*, 4 vols., edited A. C. FRASER. Oxford, 1901.

With other writings, edited A. D. LINDSAY. London, 1910.

Russian translation by A. O. MAKOWELSKY. Kazan, 1912.

With *The Theory of Vision or Visual Language*, German translation, edited R. SCHMIDT. Leipzig, 1912.

Italian translation by GIOVANNI AMENDOLA. Lanciano, 1920.

With other writings, edited MARY W. CALKINS. New York, 1929.

---

[1] I am indebted to Mr. Patrick Singleton, of the Baillieu Library, University of Melbourne, for his valuable assistance in checking several bibliographical references, here and in the notes.

In *Oeuvres Choisies,* French translation, edited ANDRÉ-LOUIS LEROY. Paris, 1943.

With *Principles,* Spanish translation, edited FELIPE GONŹALEZ VINCEN. Buenos Aires, 1948.

In *Works,* 9 vols., edited A. A. LUCE AND T. E. JESSOP. Edinburgh, 1948-57.

The Theory of Vision or Visual Language

EDITION PUBLISHED BY BERKELEY

London, 1733.

POSTHUMOUS EDITIONS

Edited H. V. H. COWELL. London, 1860.

In *Works,* edited A. C. FRASER. Oxford, 1871.

In *Works,* edited G. SAMPSON. London, 1897-8.

In *Works,* edited A. C. FRASER. Oxford, 1901.

With *Essay,* German translation, edited R. SCHMIDT. Leipzig, 1912.

In *Works,* edited A. A. LUCE AND T. E. JESSOP. Edinburgh, 1948-57.

2. WORKS WITH DIRECT REFERENCE TO BERKELEY'S THEORY

ABBOTT, THOMAS K. *Sight and Touch: An Attempt to Disprove the Received (or Berkeleian) Theory of Vision.* London, 1864.

ARMSTRONG, DAVID M. *Berkeley's Theory of Vision: A Critical Examination of Bishop Berkeley's Essay towards a New Theory of Vision.* Melbourne: Melbourne University Press, 1961.

BAILEY, SAMUEL. *A Review of Berkeley's Theory of Vision, designed to show the unsoundness of that celebrated speculation.* London, 1842.

LUCE, A. A. *Berkeley and Malebranche.* Oxford, 1934.

MILL, J. S. *Dissertations and Discussions.* Vol. II. London, 1859.

PIRENNE, M. H. "Physiological Mechanisms in the Perception of Distance by Sight and Berkeley's Theory of Vision," *British Journal for the Philosophy of Science,* IV, 13 (May, 1953), 13-21.

RASMUSSEN, E. TRANEKJAER. "Berkeley and Modern Psychology," *British Journal for the Philosophy of Science,* IV, 13 (May, 1953), 2-12.

TURBAYNE, COLIN MURRAY. *The Myth of Metaphor.* New Haven and London: Yale University Press, 1962.

WARNOCK, G. J. *Berkeley.* "Penguin Books." London, 1953.

3. WORKS WITH SPECIAL BEARING UPON BERKELEY'S THEORY

ARISTOTLE. *De Anima.*

CARNAP, RUDOLF. *Der Logische Aufbau der Welt.* Berlin: Weltkreis Verlag, 1928.

CONDILLAC, E. B. DE. *Essai sur l'origine des connaissances humaines.* Amsterdam, 1746.

———. *Traité des sensations.* London and Paris, 1754. Translated by G. CARR. London, 1930.

DESCARTES, RENÉ. *La dioptrique,* appended to *Discours de la méthode.* Paris, 1637.

DIDEROT, DENIS. *Lettre sur les aveugles.* London, 1749.

GIBSON, JAMES J. *The Perception of the Visual World.* Boston: Houghton Mifflin, 1950.

GOODMAN, NELSON. *The Structure of Appearance.* Cambridge: Harvard University Press, 1951.

———. "The Way the World Is," *Review of Metaphysics,* XIV, 1 (September, 1960), 48-56.

GOMBRICH, E. H. *Art and Illusion; a Study in the Psychology of Pictorial Representation.* New York: Pantheon Books, 1960.

HAYEK, F. A. *The Sensory Order.* London: Routledge & Kegan Paul, 1952.

HEBB, D. O. *The Organization of Behavior: A Neuropsychological Theory.* New York: Wiley, 1949.

HELMHOLTZ, HERMANN L. F. VON. *Handbuch der physiologischen Optik.* Hamburg and Leipzig, 1856. See *Helmholtz's Treatise on Physiological Optics,* translated from the 3rd German edition by JAMES P. SOUTHALL, Vol. III, *The Perceptions of Vision.* Rochester: The Optical Society of America, 1925.

MALEBRANCHE, NICHOLAS. *De la recherche de la vérité.* Paris, 1674.

PLATO. *Cratylus.*

———. *Theaetetus.*

REID, THOMAS. *Inquiry into the Human Mind on the Principles of Common Sense.* Edinburgh and Dublin, 1764.

RONCHI, VASCO. *Optics: The Science of Vision.* New York: New York University Press, 1957. Translated by EDWARD ROSEN from *L'Ottica Scienza Della Visione.* Bologna, 1955.

RUSSELL, BERTRAND. *An Inquiry into Meaning and Truth.* London: Allen & Unwin, 1940.

SENDEN, MARIUS VON. *Space and Sight.* Glencoe, Ill.: The Free Press, 1960. Translated by PETER HEATH from *Raum und Gestaltauffassung bei operierten Blindgeborenen vor und nach der operation.* Leipzig, 1932.

VOLTAIRE, F. M. A. DE. *Éclaircissements sur les éléments de la philosophie de Newton.* Paris, 1738.

NOTE ON THE TEXTS

The texts printed here are those of Berkeley's final editions, except that I have restored the Dedication of the *Essay Towards a New Theory of Vision,* which Berkeley omitted from the third and fourth editions, and the Appendix to the *Essay,* peculiar to the second edition. All other significant differences between the editions are given in the footnotes, using Roman numerals to refer to the different editions.

The text of the three sections from *A Treatise Concerning the Principles of Human Knowledge* is that of the second and last edition, published in London in 1734, the first edition having appeared in Dublin in 1710. The text of the *Essay* is that of Berkeley's fourth and last edition of 1732, which was annexed to the second London edition of *Alciphron.* Previous editions were: I, 1709, Dublin; II, 1709 (Old Style, probably February, 1710), Dublin; III, 1732, annexed to the first edition of *Alciphron.* The text of the excerpts from the Fourth Dialogue of *Alciphron* is that of the third London edition of 1752, previous editions having been: I, 1732, Dublin and London, with the third edition of *Essay* annexed; and II, also 1732, London, with the fourth edition of the *Essay* annexed. Another edition, styled "Third," a careless reprint of the first, appeared in London in 1732. The text of *Visual Language* is that of Berkeley's only edition of 1733, which appeared in London with the anonymous letter of the *Daily Post-Boy* of September 9, 1732, appended.

The differences between the editions of each of these works are not highly significant. The most important additions to the second and subsequent editions of the *Essay* are the long passages in sections 73 and 77 where Berkeley spells out the application of his contextual theory of meaning to the solution of the Moon Illusion. In the second edition, another important addition, later omitted, is the Appendix, which clarifies both the nature of the Geometrical Theory Berkeley tries to refute and his own account of the *minimum visibile*. In footnotes to the Appendix, I have added English translations of the Latin passages that Berkeley quoted from Descartes' *Dioptrics* and Gassendi's *The Apparent Size of the Sun*. . . . For the translation of the latter passage I am indebted to Professor Elmer G. Suhr of the University of Rochester. But perhaps the most interesting alteration is Berkeley's explicit extension of the language metaphor the whole way. In the 1709 editions of the *Essay*, section 147 described the proper objects of vision as constituting "the universal language of nature"; twenty-one years later in the 1732 editions he describes them as constituting "a universal language of the Author of nature."

Spelling, punctuation, and capitalization have been revised to conform to present-day American usage.

C.M.T.

WORKS ON VISION

A TREATISE CONCERNING
THE PRINCIPLES OF HUMAN KNOWLEDGE

THE THIRD OBJECTION [1]

42. *Thirdly,* it will be objected that we see things actually without or at a distance from us, and which, consequently, do not exist in the mind, it being absurd that those things which are seen at the distance of several miles should be as near to us as our own thoughts.[2] In answer to this I desire it may be considered that in a dream we do oft perceive things as existing at a great distance off, and yet for all that those things are acknowledged to have their existence only in the mind.

43. But, for the fuller clearing of this point, it may be worthwhile to consider how it is that we perceive distance, and things placed at a distance, by sight. For that we should in truth see external space, and bodies actually existing in it, some nearer, others farther off, seems to carry with it some opposition to what has been said of their existing nowhere without the mind. The consideration of this difficulty it was that gave birth to my *Essay Towards a New Theory of Vision,*[3]

1 [I.e., the third of the thirteen objections that Berkeley anticipates will be made against his immaterialism. Most of his anticipations have since been proved correct.]

2 [Cf. Malebranche: "Men have always consulted their eyes to be assured of the existence of matter" (*The Search after Truth,* T. Taylor translation [Oxford, 1694], from *De la recherche de la vérité* [Paris, 1674], Illustration to Bk. I, chap. x).]

3 [Cf. A. A. Luce: "The *Essay* sprang from the *Principles* and not vice versa" (*Berkeley's Immaterialism* [Edinburgh, 1946], p. 7); and T. E. Jessop: "Berkeley's immaterialism preceded his theory of vision, as is clear from the *Philosophical Commentaries* as now edited" (*The Works of George Berkeley, Bishop of Cloyne,* ed. A. A. Luce and T. E. Jessop, II [Edinburgh, 1949], 58, note 1). A. C. Fraser held the opposite view: "The theory of vision was the seminal principle of Berkeley's theory of matter" (*Berkeley's Complete Works,* I [Oxford, 1901], 114). For one solution to

3

which was published not long since, wherein it is shown that distance or outness is neither immediately of itself perceived by sight,[4] nor yet apprehended or judged of by lines and angles, or anything that has a necessary connection with it; [5] but that it is only suggested to our thoughts by certain visible ideas and sensations attending vision, which in their own nature have no manner of similitude or relation either with distance or things placed at a distance; [6] but by a connection taught us by experience they come to signify and suggest them to us after the same manner that words of any language suggest the ideas they are made to stand for; [7] insomuch that a man born blind and afterward made to see would not, at first sight, think the things he saw to be without his mind or at any distance from him. See sec. 41 of the forementioned treatise.

44. The ideas of sight and touch make two species entirely distinct and heterogeneous.[8] The former are marks and prognostics of the latter. That the proper objects of sight neither exist without the mind, nor are the images of external things, was shown even in that treatise.[9] Though throughout the same the contrary be supposed true of tangible objects—not that to suppose that vulgar error [10] was necessary for establishing the notion therein laid down, but because it was beside my purpose to examine and refute it in a discourse concerning *vision*. So that in strict truth the ideas of sight,[11] when we

---

this complex problem see my article, "The Influence of Berkeley's Science on His Metaphysics," *Philosophy and Phenomenological Research*, XVI, 4 (June, 1956), 476-87.]

4 [*Essay*, sec. 2.]   5 [*Essay*, secs. 11-15.]
6 [*Essay*, secs. 3, 16-28.]   7 [*Essay*, sec. 51.]
8 [*Essay*, secs. 47-49, 121-46.]   9 [*Essay*, sec. 43.]

10 [*Essay*, secs. 55, 94, 111, etc. See Editor's Commentary, sec. 8, p. xliv.]

11 [I.e., the proper, primary, or immediate objects of sight, i.e., those objects immediately perceived, or sensed, by sight, namely, "variety of lights and colors," which have their own peculiar size, shape, motion, and position in the visual field, but which lack distance both between themselves and from the eye of the observer. See *Essay*, secs. 77, 103, 127, 129, etc., and *Visual Language*, secs. 10, 11, 41. Cf. Aristotle: "By a proper ob-

apprehend by them distance and things placed at a distance, do not suggest or mark out to us things actually existing at a distance, but only admonish us what ideas of touch [12] will be imprinted in our minds at such and such distances of time, and in consequence of such and such actions. It is, I say, evident, from what has been said in the foregoing parts of this treatise, and in sec. 147 and elsewhere of the *Essay Concerning Vision*, that visible ideas are the language whereby the Governing Spirit on whom we depend informs us what tangible ideas he is about to imprint upon us, in case we excite this or that motion in our own bodies. But for a fuller information in this point I refer to the *Essay* itself.

---

ject I mean one that cannot be sensed by any other sense and in respect of which no error [or truth] is possible. Thus color is the proper object of sight, . . . " (*De Anima* 418a).]

[12] [Includes muscular and locomotive ideas. This sentence manifests the full immaterialism of the *Principles* as opposed to the partial immaterialism of the *Essay*. The latter reveals an immaterialism only of sight and, perhaps, of sound. In the *Essay* tactual objects are allowed "to exist without (the) mind in the ambient space" (*Essay*, sec. 94). The word "admonish" characterizes the directive or pragmatic function of language, the importance of which Berkeley constantly stresses. See Editor's Commentary, sec. 8, p. xliv.]

AN ESSAY TOWARDS
A NEW THEORY OF VISION

TO THE
RT. HON. SIR JOHN PERCIVALE, BART.[1]

*One of Her Majesty's Most Honorable
Privy Council in the Kingdom of Ireland* [2]

SIR,

I could not, without doing violence to myself, forbear upon
this occasion to give some public testimony of the great and
well grounded esteem I have conceived for you, ever since I
had the honor and happiness of your acquaintance. The outward advantages of fortune, and the early honors with which
you are adorned, together with the reputation you are known
to have among the best and most considerable men, may well
imprint veneration and esteem on the minds of those who behold you from a distance. But these are not the chief motives
that inspire me with the respect I bear you. A nearer approach
has given me the view of something in your person infinitely
beyond the external ornaments of honor and estate. I mean
an intrinsic stock of virtue and good sense, a true concern for
religion, and disinterested love of your country. Add to these
uncommon proficiency in the best and most useful parts of
knowledge, together with (what in my mind is a perfection of
the first rank) a surpassing goodness of nature. All which I

---

[1] [I.e., Baronet. Created Earl of Egmont in 1733, Percival (1683-1748)
was Berkeley's friend for about forty years, and one of his two principal
correspondents. For the Berkeley-Percival correspondence, see B. Rand's
Berkeley and Percival (Cambridge, 1914).]

[2] [The Dedication was omitted from the third and fourth editions.]

have collected, not from the uncertain reports of fame, but from my own experience. Within these few months that I have the honor to be known unto you, the many delightful hours I have passed in your agreeable and improving conversation have afforded me the opportunity of discovering in you many excellent qualities which at once fill me with admiration and esteem. That one at those years, and in those circumstances of wealth and greatness, should continue proof against the charms of luxury and those criminal pleasures so fashionable and predominant in the age we live in; that he should preserve a sweet and modest behavior, free from that insolent and assuming air so familiar to those who are placed above the ordinary rank of men; that he should manage a great fortune with that prudence and inspection,[3] and at the same time expend it with that generosity and nobleness of mind, as to show himself equally remote from a sordid parsimony and a lavish, inconsiderate profusion of the good things he is entrusted with—this, surely, were admirable and praiseworthy. But that he should, moreover, by an impartial exercise of his reason and constant perusal of the sacred Scriptures, endeavor to attain a right notion of the principles of natural and revealed religion; that he should with the concern of a true patriot have the interest of the public at heart, and omit no means of informing himself what may be prejudicial or advantageous to his country, in order to prevent the one and promote the other; in fine, that, by a constant application to the most severe and useful studies, by a strict observation of the rules of honor and virtue, by frequent and serious reflections on the mistaken measures of the world and the true end and happiness of mankind, he should in all respects qualify himself bravely to run the race that is set before him, to deserve the character of great and good in this life, and be ever happy hereafter—this were amazing and almost incredible. Yet all this, and more than this, Sir, might I justly say of you, did either your modesty permit, or your character stand in need of it. I know it might deservedly be

3 [Inspection—I: circumspection.]

thought a vanity in me to imagine that anything coming from so obscure a hand as mine could add a luster to your reputation. But I am withal sensible how far I advance the interest of my own by laying hold on this opportunity to make it known that I am admitted into some degree of intimacy with a person of your exquisite judgment. And, with that view, I have ventured to make you an address of this nature, which the goodness I have ever experienced in you inclines me to hope will meet with a favorable reception at your hands. Though I must own I have your pardon to ask for touching on what may possibly be offensive to a virtue you are possessed of in a very distinguishing degree. Excuse me, Sir, if it was out of my power to mention the name of Sir John Percivale without paying some tribute to that extraordinary and surprising merit whereof I have so clear and affecting an idea, and which, I am sure, cannot be exposed in too full a light for the imitation of others.

Of late I have been agreeably employed in considering the most noble, pleasant, and comprehensive of all the ser_ses.[4] The fruit of that (labor shall I call it or) diversion is what I now present you with, in hopes it may give some entertainment to one who, in the midst of business and vulgar enjoyments, preserves a relish for the more refined pleasures of thought and reflection. My thoughts concerning vision have led me into some notions so far out of the common road that it had been improper to address them to one of a narrow and contracted genius. But, you, Sir, being master of a large and

---

4 [Cf. Malebranche: "Sight is the first, the most noble, and the most comprehensive of all the senses" (*The Search*, Bk. I, chap. vi); and "To understand well how we see objects is to be ready for the discovery of an infinite number of truths, not only in physics but also in metaphysics, concerning the nature of ideas, of goodness, of generality, and of the incomprehensible wisdom of divine providence" (*The Search*, Last Illustration). Similar remarks are made by Locke (*Essay* [Oxford, 1689], Bk. II, chap. ix, sec. 9), by Descartes (*Dioptrics* [Paris, 1637], Discourse I, and *Principles* [Paris, 1644], Part IV, sec. 195), and by Aristotle: "[Our senses] are loved for themselves; and above all others, the sense of sight" (*Metaphysics* I. i), and: "Sight is the most highly developed sense" (*De Anima* 429a).]

free understanding, raised above the power of those prejudices
that enslave the far greater part of mankind, may deservedly
be thought a proper patron for an attempt of this kind. Add
to this that you are no less disposed to forgive than qualified
to discern whatever faults may occur in it. Nor do I think
you defective in any one point necessary to form an exact
judgment on the most abstract and difficult things, so much
as in a just confidence of your own abilities. And in this one
instance, give me leave to say, you show a manifest weakness
of judgment. With relation to the following essay, I shall only
add that I beg your pardon for laying a trifle of that nature
in your way, at a time when you are engaged in the important
affairs of the nation, and desire you to think that I am, with
all sincerity and respect,

Sir,

Your most faithful and most humble servant,

GEORGE BERKELEY

CONTENTS

138. The way wherein we apprehend motion by sight easily collected from what has been said

139. *Q.* How visible and tangible ideas came to have the same name, if not of the same kind

140. This accounted for without supposing them of the same kind

141. *Obj.* That a tangible square is liker to a visible square than to a visible circle

142. *Ans.* That a visible square is fitter than a visible circle to represent a tangible square

143. But it does not hence follow that a visible square is like a tangible square

144. Why we are more apt to confound visible with tangible ideas than other signs with the things signified

145. Several other reasons hereof assigned

146. Reluctancy in rejecting any opinion no argument of its truth

147. Proper objects of vision the language of the Author of nature [5]

148. In it there is much admirable and deserving our attention

149. Question proposed concerning the object of geometry

150. At first view we are apt to think visible extension the object of geometry

151. Visible extension shown not to be the object of geometry

152. Words may as well be thought the object of geometry as visible extension

153. It is proposed to inquire what progress an intelligence that could see, but not feel, might make in geometry

154. He cannot understand those parts which relate to solids, and their surfaces, and lines generated by their section

155. Nor even the elements of plane geometry

[5] [The language of the Author of nature—I, II: the language of nature.]

156. The proper objects of sight incapable of being managed as geometrical figures

157. The opinion of those who hold plane figures to be the immediate objects of sight considered

158. Planes no more the immediate objects of sight than solids

159. Difficult to enter precisely into the thoughts of the above-mentioned intelligence [6]

[6] [Intelligence—I, II add here another section: 160. The object of geometry, its not being sufficiently understood, cause of difficulty and useless labor in that science.]

AN ESSAY TOWARDS
A NEW THEORY OF VISION

1. My design is to show the manner wherein we perceive by sight the distance, magnitude, and situation of objects.[7] Also to consider the difference there is betwixt the ideas of sight and touch, and whether there be any idea common to both senses.[8]

2. It is, I think, agreed by all that distance, of itself and immediately, cannot be seen.[9] For, distance being a line directed endwise to the eye, it projects only one point in the fund of the eye, which point remains invariably the same, whether the distance be longer or shorter.[10]

7 [This "analysis" (see *Visual Language,* sec. 38) occupies secs. 2-120.]

8 [Both senses—I: both senses. In treating of all which, it seems to me, the writers of optics have proceeded on wrong principles. Secs. 121-46. Berkeley reaches the conclusion of his analysis in secs. 147-48 and then draws a corollary in secs. 149-59.]

9 [How we perceive by sight the distance of objects is analyzed in secs. 2-51. Cf. *Alciphron,* Dial. IV, secs. 8-9; *Visual Language,* secs. 62-68; *Three Dialogues,* I.]

10 [The view that "distance, of itself and immediately, cannot be seen" is considered by some critics to be a central contribution of Berkeley, the premise of the conclusions of the theory of vision, and the argument for it—Berkeley's only one—invalid. See, e.g., Samuel Bailey's *Review of Berkeley's Theory of Vision* (London, 1842), pp. 38-43; Thomas K. Abbott's *Sight and Touch* (London, 1864), pp. 9-12; and David M. Armstrong's *Berkeley's Theory of Vision* (Melbourne, 1961), pp. xiii, 9-15. Mill defends it in his *Dissertations and Discussions* (London, 1859), II, 172-74. The view, however, is not Berkeley's own although he does accept this much of the received theory, summarized in secs. 2-7, most of it expressed in Molyneux's *New Dioptrics* (London, 1692), p. 113, e.g., "Distance of itself is not to be perceived. For it is a line (or a length) presented to our eye with its end toward us, which must therefore be only a point, and that is invisible." Berkeley and the optical theorists deny not that we can tell by sight the distance of objects but that we sense it (sec. 11). Berkeley's contribution here is his account of the manner in which we tell the distance of near objects by sight. The view, accepted both by Berkeley and his opponents, that distance is not immediately seen is a conclusion, not a premise, of his theory of vision.]

3. I find it also acknowledged that the estimate we make of the distance of objects considerably remote is rather an act of judgment grounded on experience than of sense. For example, when I perceive a great number of intermediate objects, such as houses, fields, rivers, and the like, which I have experienced to take up a considerable space, I thence form a judgment or conclusion that the object I see beyond them is at a great distance. Again, when an object appears faint and small which at a near distance I have experienced to make a vigorous and large appearance, I instantly conclude it to be far off. And this, it is evident, is the result of experience without which, from the faintness and littleness, I should not have inferred anything concerning the distance of objects.

4. But, when an object is placed at so near a distance as that the interval between the eyes bears any sensible proportion to it, the opinion of speculative men is [11] that the two optic axes (the fancy that we see only with one eye at once being exploded), concurring at the object, do there make an angle,[12] by means of which, according as it is greater or lesser, the object is perceived to be nearer or farther off.[13]

5. Betwixt which and the foregoing manner of estimating distance there is this remarkable difference: that whereas there was no apparent necessary connection between small distance and a large and strong appearance, or between great distance and a little and faint appearance, there appears a very necessary connection between an obtuse angle and near distance, and an acute angle and farther distance. It does not in the least depend upon experience, but may be evidently known by anyone before he had experienced it, that the nearer the concurrence of the optic axes, the greater the angle, and the

11 [The opinion of speculative men is—I: it is the received opinion—II: it is the opinion of some.]

12 [I.e., convergence. Cf. Descartes' *Dioptrics* (1637), Discourse VI, sec. 13, translated in note 3 to Appendix of *Essay*, p. 99. Others include Johannes Kepler (*Supplement to Witelo* [Frankfurt, 1604], III, 8) and Malebranche (*The Search*, Bk. I, chap. ix, sec. 3).]

13 See what Descartes and others have written on this subject. [I and II omit this footnote.]

remoter their concurrence is, the lesser will be the angle comprehended by them.

6. There is another way, mentioned by optic writers, whereby they will have us judge of those distances in respect of which the breadth of the pupil has any sensible bigness. And that is the greater or lesser divergency of the rays which, issuing from the visible point, do fall on the pupil—that point being judged nearest which is seen by most diverging rays, and that remoter which is seen by less diverging rays, and so on; the apparent distance still increasing, as the divergency of the rays decreases, till at length it becomes infinite, when the rays that fall on the pupil are to sense parallel. And after this manner it is said we perceive distance when we look only with one eye.[14]

7. In this case also it is plain we are not beholden to experience, it being a certain necessary truth that the nearer the direct rays falling on the eye approach to a parallelism, the farther off is the point of their intersection, or the visible point from whence they flow.

8. Now though the accounts here given of perceiving *near* distance by sight are received for true,[15] and accordingly made use of [16] in determining the apparent places of objects, they do nevertheless seem very unsatisfactory, and that for these following reasons:

9. It is evident that, when the mind perceives any idea not immediately and of itself, it must be by the means of some other idea. Thus, for instance, the passions which are in the mind of another are of themselves to me invisible. I may nevertheless perceive them by sight; though not immediately, yet

14 [I.e., accommodation. Cf. Descartes' *Dioptrics,* Bk. VI, and Kepler's *Supplement,* III. ix: "In vision with one eye we are able to use the distance-measuring triangle (*triangulum distantiae mensorium*) which has its vertex in the point of the object and its base in the width of the pupil."]

15 [Received for true—II: received for true by some.]

16 [8. Now though the accounts . . . made use of—I: 8. I have here set down the common, current accounts that are given of our perceiving near distances by sight, which though they are unquestionably received for true by mathematicians, and accordingly made use of by them.]

by means of the colors they produce in the countenance. We
often see shame or fear in the looks of a man by perceiving
the changes of his countenance to red or pale.

10. Moreover, it is evident that no idea which is not itself
perceived can be the means of perceiving any other idea.[17] If
I do not perceive the redness or paleness of a man's face themselves, it is impossible I should perceive by them the passions
which are in his mind.

11. Now, from sec. 2 it is plain that distance is in its own
nature imperceptible, and yet it is perceived by sight.[18] It
remains, therefore, that it be brought into view by means of
some other idea that is itself immediately perceived in the
act of vision.

12. But those lines and angles by means whereof some
men [19] pretend to explain the perception of distance are themselves not at all perceived; nor are they in truth ever thought
of by those unskillful in optics. I appeal to anyone's experience whether, upon sight of an object, he computes its distance by the bigness of the angle made by the meeting of the
two optic axes? Or whether he ever thinks of the greater or
lesser divergency of the rays which arrive from any point to his
pupil? [20] Everyone is himself the best judge of what he perceives and what not. In vain shall any man [21] tell me that I
perceive certain lines and angles which introduce into my
mind the various ideas of distance so long as I myself am
conscious of no such thing.

[17] [The first implicit use of the language model which prescribes that
signs are noticeable, contrary to the received theory in which the means
need not be noticeable. Cf. *Alciphron,* Dial. IV, sec. 8, and Descartes'
Dioptrics, Bk. VI.]

[18] [Note here the systematic ambiguity of "to perceive" used throughout meaning (1) "to sense" or (2) "to perceive" in the etymological sense,
viz., "to take (something) through (something else)."]

[19] [Some men—I: mathematicians.]

[20] [His pupil?—I: his pupil? Nay, whether it be not perfectly impossible
for him to perceive by sense the various angles wherewith the rays according to their greater or less divergence do fall on his eye.]

[21] [Any man—I: all the mathematicians in the world.]

13. Since, therefore, those angles and lines are not themselves perceived by sight, it follows, from sec. 10, that the mind does not by them judge of the distance of objects.

14. The truth of this assertion will be yet further evident to anyone that considers those lines and angles have no real existence in nature, being only a hypothesis [22] framed by the mathematicians, and by them introduced into optics that they might treat of that science in a geometrical way.

15. The last reason I shall give for rejecting that doctrine is that though we should grant the real existence of those optic angles, etc., and that it was possible for the mind to perceive them, yet these principles would not be found sufficient to explain the phenomena of distance, as shall be shown hereafter.

16. Now, it being already shown that distance is suggested [23] to the mind by the mediation of some other idea which is itself perceived in the act of seeing, it remains that we inquire what ideas or sensations there be that attend vision, unto which we may suppose the ideas of distance are connected and by which they are introduced into the mind. And, *first,* it is certain by experience that when we look at a near object with both eyes, according as it approaches or recedes from us, we alter the disposition of our eyes by lessening or widening the interval between the pupils. This disposition or turn of the eyes is attended with a sensation [24] which seems to me to be that which in this case brings the idea of greater or lesser distance into the mind.

17. Not that there is any natural or necessary connection between the sensation we perceive by the turn of the eyes and greater or lesser distance. But—because the mind has, by con-

22 [Cf. *De Motu,* secs. 17, 18, 39, 66, etc.; *Alciphron,* Dial. VII, sec. 9; *Siris,* sec. 250: "Mechanic philosophers and geometricians . . . take mathematical hypotheses for real beings. . . ."]

23 [First use of this important term expressing the relation between the sign and the thing signified. Cf. *Alciphron,* Dial. IV, sec. 9; *Visual Language,* sec. 42.]

24 [I.e., of touch. Cf. *Essay,* sec. 145; *Visual Language,* sec. 66.]

stant experience, found the different sensations corresponding
to the different dispositions of the eyes to be attended each
with a different degree of distance in the object—there has
grown a habitual or customary connection between those two
sorts of ideas so that the mind no sooner perceives the sensation arising from the different turn it gives the eyes, in order
to bring the pupils nearer or farther asunder, but it withal
perceives the different idea of distance which was wont to be
connected with that sensation. Just as, upon hearing a certain
sound, the idea is immediately suggested to the understanding
which custom had united with it.

18. Nor do I see how I can easily be mistaken in this matter. I know evidently that distance is not perceived of itself;
that, by consequence, it must be perceived by means of some
other idea which is immediately perceived, and varies with the
different degrees of distance. I know also that the sensation
arising from the turn of the eyes is of itself immediately perceived; and various degrees thereof are connected with different distances, which never fail to accompany them into my
mind, when I view an object distinctly with both eyes whose
distance is so small that in respect of it the interval between
the eyes has any considerable magnitude.

19. I know it is a received opinion that, by altering the disposition of the eyes, the mind perceives whether the angle of
the optic axes or the lateral angles comprehended between the
interval of the eyes and the optic axes are [25] made greater or
lesser; and that, accordingly, by a kind of natural geometry, it
judges the point of their intersection to be nearer or farther
off. But that this is not true I am convinced by my own experience; since I am not conscious that I make any such use
of the perception I have by the turn of my eyes. And for me
to make those judgments and draw those conclusions from it,
without knowing that I do so, seems altogether incomprehensible.

20. From all which it follows that the judgment we make
of the distance of an object viewed with both eyes is entirely
the result of experience. If we had not constantly found cer-

25 [Or the lateral angles . . . optic axes are—I, II: is.]

tain sensations, arising from the various disposition of the eyes, attended with certain degrees of distance, we should never make those sudden judgments from them concerning the distance of objects; no more than we would pretend to judge of a man's thoughts by his pronouncing words we had never heard before.

21. *Secondly,* an object placed at a certain distance from the eye, to which the breadth of the pupil bears a considerable proportion, being made to approach, is seen more confusedly.[26] And the nearer it is brought the more confused appearance it makes. And this being found constantly to be so, there arises in the mind a habitual connection between the several degrees of confusion and distance, the greater confusion still implying the lesser distance and the lesser confusion the greater distance of the object.

22. This confused appearance of the object does therefore seem to be the medium whereby the mind judges of distance in those cases wherein the most approved writers of optics will have it judge by the different divergency with which the rays flowing from the radiating point fall on the pupil. No man, I believe, will pretend to see or feel those imaginary angles that the rays are supposed to form according to their various inclinations on his eye. But he cannot choose seeing whether the object appear more or less confused. It is therefore a manifest consequence from what has been demonstrated that, instead of the greater or lesser divergency of the rays, the mind makes use of the greater or lesser confusedness of the appearance, thereby to determine the apparent place of an object.

23. Nor does it avail to say there is not any necessary connection between confused vision and distance great or small. For I ask any man what necessary connection he sees between the redness of a blush and shame? And yet no sooner shall he behold that color to arise in the face of another but it brings into his mind the idea of that passion which has been observed to accompany it.

24. What seems to have misled the writers of optics in this

[26] [Cf. sec. 35.]

matter is that they imagine men judge of distance as they do of a conclusion in mathematics; betwixt which and the premises it is indeed absolutely requisite there be an apparent necessary connection. But it is far otherwise in the sudden judgments men make of distance. We are not to think that brutes and children, or even grown reasonable men, whenever they perceive an object to approach or depart from them, do it by virtue of geometry and demonstration.

25. That one idea may suggest another to the mind, it will suffice that they have been observed to go together, without any demonstration of the necessity of their coexistence or without so much as knowing what makes them so to coexist. Of this there are innumerable instances, of which no one can be ignorant.

26. Thus, greater confusion having been constantly attended with nearer distance, no sooner is the former idea perceived but it suggests the latter to our thoughts. And, if it had been the ordinary course of nature that the farther off an object were placed the more confused it should appear, it is certain the very same perception that now makes us think an object approaches would then have made us to imagine it went farther off, that perception, abstracting from custom and experience, being equally fitted to produce the idea of great distance, or small distance, or no distance at all.

27. *Thirdly,* an object being placed at the distance above specified, and brought nearer to the eye, we may nevertheless prevent, at least for some time, the appearance's growing more confused by straining the eye. In which case that sensation supplies the place of confused vision in aiding the mind to judge of the distance of the object, it being esteemed so much the nearer by how much the effort or straining of the eye in order to distinct vision is greater.

28. I have here set down those sensations or ideas that seem to be the constant and general occasions of introducing into the mind the different ideas of near distance. It is true, in most cases, that divers other circumstances contribute to frame our idea of distance, viz., the particular number, size,

kind, etc., of the things seen. Concerning which, as well as all other the forementioned occasions which suggest distance, I shall only observe, they have none of them, in their own nature, any relation or connection with it; nor is it possible they should ever signify the various degrees thereof otherwise than as by experience they have been found to be connected with them.

29. I shall proceed upon these principles to account for a phenomenon which has hitherto strangely puzzled the writers of optics, and is so far from being accounted for by any of their theories of vision that it is, by their own confession, plainly repugnant to them, and of consequence, if nothing else could be objected, were alone sufficient to bring their credit in question. The whole difficulty I shall lay before you in the words of the learned Doctor Barrow [27] with which he concludes his optic lectures:

> Haec sunt, quae circa partem opticae praecipue mathematicam dicenda mihi suggessit meditatio. Circa reliquas (quae φυσικώτεραι sunt, adeoque saepiuscule pro certis principiis plausibiles conjecturas venditare necessum habent) nihil fere quicquam admodum verisimile succurrit, a pervulgatis (ab iis, inquam, quae Keplerus, Scheinerus, Cartesius, et post illos alii tradiderunt) alienum aut diversum. Atqui tacere malo, quam toties oblatam crambem reponere. Proinde receptui cano; nec ita tamen ut prorsus discedam, anteaquam improbam quandam difficultatem (pro sinceritate quam et vobis et veritati debeo minime dissimulandam) in medium protulero, quae doctrinae nostrae, hactenus inculcatae, se objicit adversam, ab ea saltem nullam admittit solutionem. Illa, breviter, talis est. *Lenti vel speculo cavo EBF* exponatur punctum visibile *A*, ita distans, ut radii ex *A* manantes ex inflectione versus axem *AB* cogantur. Sitque radiationis limes (seu puncti *A* imago, qualem supra passim

[27] [Isaac Barrow (1630-77), Newton's teacher at Cambridge and his predecessor in the Lucasian chair of mathematics. The extract is from *Eighteen Lectures* (London, 1669), Lect. 18. For other statements of Barrow's difficulty, see Molyneux's *New Dioptrics*, Part I, prop. 31, sec. 9; Robert Smith's *A Compleat System of Opticks* (Cambridge, 1738), Vol. II, Remarks on article 138; Vasco Ronchi's *Optics: The Science of Vision* (New York, 1957), secs. 141, 170, 190, 193.]

statuimus) punctum Z. Inter hoc autem et inflectentis verticem B uspiam positus concipiatur oculus. Quaeri jam potest, ubi loci debeat punctum A apparere? Retrorsum ad punctum Z videri non fert natura (cum omnis impressio sensum afficiens proveniat a partibus A) ac experientia reclamat. Nostris autem e placitis consequi videtur, ipsum ad partes anticas apparens, ab intervallo longissime dissito (quod et maximum sensibile quodvis intervallum quodammodo exsuperet), apparere. Cum enim quo radiis minus divergentibus attingitur objectum, eo (seclusis utique praenotionibus et praejudiciis) longius abesse sentiatur; et quod parallelos ad oculum radios projicit, remotissime positum aestimetur. Exigere ratio videtur, ut quod convergentibus radiis apprehenditur, adhuc magis, si fieri posset, quoad apparentiam elongetur. Quin et circa casum hunc generatim inquiri possit, quidnam omnino sit, quod apparentem puncti A locum determinet, faciatque quod constanti ratione nunc propius, nunc remotius appareat? Cui itidem dubio nihil quicquam ex hactenus dictorum analogia responderi posse videtur, nisi debere punctum A perpetuo longissime semotum videri. Verum experientia secus attestatur, illud pro diversa oculi inter puncta B, Z, positione varie distans, nunquam fere (si unquam) longinquius ipso A libere spectato, subinde vero multo propinquius adparere; quinimo, quo oculum appellentes radii magis convergunt, eo speciem objecti propius accedere. Nempe, si puncto B admoveatur *oculus,* suo (ad lentem) fere nativo in loco conspicitur punctum A (vel aeque distans, ad *speculum*); ad O reductus oculus ejusce speciem appropinquantem cernit; ad P adhuc vicinius ipsum existimat; ac ita sensim, donec alicubi tandem, velut ad Q, constituto oculo, objectum summe propinquum apparens in meram confusionem incipiat evanescere. Quae sane cuncta rationibus atque decretis nostris repugnare videntur, aut cum iis saltem parum amice conspirant. Neque nostram tantum sententiam pulsat hoc experimentum; at ex aequo caeteras quas norim omnes, veterem imprimis ac vulgatam,

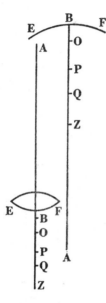

nostrae prae reliquis affinem, ita convellere videtur, ut ejus vi coactus doctissimus *A*. Tacquetus isti principio (cui pene soli totam inaedificaverat *Catoptricam* suam) ceu infido ac inconstanti renunciarit, adeoque suam ipse doctrinam labefactarit; id tamen, opinor, minime facturus, si rem totam inspexisset penitius, atque difficultatis fundum attigisset. Apud me vero non ita pollet haec, nec eousque praepollebit ulla difficultas, ut ab iis quae manifeste rationi consentanea video, discedam; praesertim quum, ut hic accidit, ejusmodi difficultas in singularis cujuspiam casus disparitate fundetur. Nimirum in praesente casu peculiare quiddam, naturae subtilitati involutum, delitescit, aegre fortassis, nisi perfectius explorato videndi modo, detegendum. Circa quod nil, fateor, hactenus excogitare potui, quod adblandiretur animo meo, nedum plane satisfaceret. Vobis itaque nodum hunc, utinam feliciore conatu, resolvendum committo.

In English as follows:

I have here delivered what my thoughts have suggested to me concerning that part of optics which is more properly mathematical. As for the other parts of that science (which, being rather physical do consequently abound with plausible conjectures instead of certain principles), there has in them scarce anything occurred to my observation different from what has been already said by Kepler, Scheinerus,[28] Descartes, and others. And methinks I had better say nothing at all than repeat that which has been so often said by others. I think it therefore high time to take my leave of this subject. But before I quit it for good and all, the fair and ingenuous dealing that I owe both to you and to truth obliges me to acquaint you with a certain untoward difficulty which seems directly opposite to the doctrine I have been hitherto inculcating, at least admits of no solution from it. In short it is this. Before the double convex glass or concave speculum *EBF*, let the point *A* be placed at such a distance that the rays proceeding from *A*, after refraction or reflection, be brought to unite somewhere in the axis *AB*. And suppose the point of

28 [Christopher Scheiner, Jesuit astronomer, one of the discoverers of sunspots, enemy of Galileo, discovered the existence of retinal images before Descartes. Cf. Descartes' *Dioptrics*, Bk. VI.]

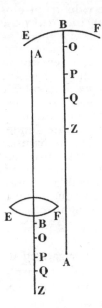

union (i.e., the image of the point *A*, as has been already set forth) to be *Z*; between which and *B*, the vertex of the glass or speculum, conceive the eye to be anywhere placed. The question now is, where the point *A* ought to appear. Experience shows that it does not appear behind at the point *Z*; and it were contrary to nature that it should; since all the impression which affects the sense comes from toward *A*. But from our tenets it should seem to follow that it would appear before the eye at a vast distance off, so great as should in some sort surpass all sensible distance. For since, if we exclude all anticipations and prejudices, every object appears by so much the farther off by how much the rays it sends to the eye are less diverging; and that object is thought to be most remote from which parallel rays proceed unto the eye; reason would make one think that object should appear at yet a greater distance which is seen by converging rays. Moreover, it may in general be asked concerning this case, what it is that determines the apparent place of the point *A*, and makes it appear after a constant manner, sometimes nearer, at other times farther off? To which doubt I see nothing that can be answered agreeable to the principles we have laid down, except only that the point *A* ought always to appear extremely remote. But, on the contrary, we are assured by experience that the point *A* appears variously distant, according to the different situations of the eye between the points *B* and *Z*. And that it does almost never (if at all) seem farther off than it would if it were beheld by the naked eye; but, on the contrary, it does sometimes appear much nearer. Nay, it is even certain that by how much the rays falling on the eye do more converge, by so much the nearer does the object seem to approach. For, the eye being placed close to the point *B*, the object *A* appears nearly in its

own natural place, if the point B is taken in the glass, or at
the same distance, if in the speculum. The eye being brought
back to O, the object seems to draw near; and, being come to
P, it beholds it still nearer; and so on by little and little, till
at length the eye being placed somewhere, suppose at Q, the
object appearing extremely near begins to vanish into mere
confusion. All which seems repugnant to our principles; at
least, not rightly to agree with them. Nor is our tenet alone
struck at by this experiment, but likewise all others that ever
came to my knowledge are every whit as much endangered by
it. The ancient one especially (which is most commonly received, and comes nearest to mine) seems to be so effectually
overthrown thereby that the most learned Tacquet [29] has been
forced to reject that principle as false and uncertain on which
alone he had built almost his whole *Catoptrics,* and consequently, by taking away the foundation, has himself pulled
down the superstructure he had raised on it. Which, nevertheless, I do not believe he would have done, had he considered
the whole matter more thoroughly and examined the difficulty
to the bottom. But as for me, neither this nor any other difficulty shall have so great an influence on me as to make me
renounce that which I know to be manifestly agreeable to
reason. Especially when, as it here falls out, the difficulty is
founded in the peculiar nature of a certain odd and particular
case. For, in the present case, something peculiar lies hid,
which, being involved in the subtlety of nature, will perhaps
hardly be discovered till such time as the manner of vision is
more perfectly made known. Concerning which I must own I
have hitherto been able to find out nothing that has the least
show of probability, not to mention certainty. I shall therefore
leave this knot to be untied by you, wishing you may have
better success in it than I have had.

[29] [Andrée Tacquet (1602-60), Jesuit mathematician, tried to retain "the
Ancient Principle," "the most fecund in all catoptrics" (vision through
mirrors): "In plane and convex mirrors, any point of the object appears
nowhere else than at the intersection of the reflected ray and the perpendicular of incidence" (*Catoptrics,* Bk. I, prop. 22, included in his *Opera*

30. The ancient and received principle which Dr. Barrow here mentions as the main foundation of Tacquet's *Catoptrics,* is that *every visible point seen by reflection from a speculum shall appear placed at the intersection of the reflected ray and the perpendicular of incidence.* Which intersection in the present case happening to be behind the eye, it greatly shakes the authority of that principle whereon the aforementioned author proceeds throughout his whole *Catoptrics* in determining the apparent place of objects seen by reflection from any kind of speculum.

31. Let us now see how this phenomenon agrees with our tenets. The eye, the nearer it is placed to the point B in the foregoing figures, the more distinct is the appearance of the object; but, as it recedes to O, the appearance grows more confused; and at P it sees the object yet more confused; and so on, till the eye, being brought back to Z, sees the object in the greatest confusion of all. Wherefore, by sec. 21, the object should seem to approach the eye gradually, as it recedes from the point B; that is, at O it should (in consequence of the principle I have laid down in the aforesaid section) seem nearer than it did at B, and at P nearer than at O, and at Q nearer than at P, and so on, till it quite vanishes at Z. Which is the very matter of fact, as anyone that pleases may easily satisfy himself by experiment.

32. This case is much the same as if we should suppose an Englishman to meet a foreigner who used the same words with the English, but in a direct contrary signification. The Englishman would not fail to make a wrong judgment of the ideas annexed to those sounds, in the mind of him that used them. Just so in the present case, the object speaks (if I may say so) with words that the eye is well acquainted with, that is, confusions of appearance; but, whereas heretofore the greater confusions were always wont to signify nearer distance, they have in this case a direct contrary signification, be-

---

Mathematica [2d. edn.; Antwerp, 1707]). The principle was enunciated by Euclid (300 B.C.) in his *Catoptrics,* theorems 16-18, and adopted by Ptolemy, Ibn al-Haitham, Witelo, Grosseteste, Roger Bacon, *et al.* See Editor's Introduction, sec. 7, note 6, p. xxxviii.]

ing connected with the greater distances. Whence it follows that the eye must unavoidably be mistaken, since it will take the confusions in the sense it has been used to, which is directly opposed to the true.

33. This phenomenon, as it entirely subverts the opinion of those who will have us judge of distance by lines and angles, on which supposition it is altogether inexplicable, so it seems to me no small confirmation of the truth of that principle whereby it is explained. But in order to a more full explication of this point, and to show how far the hypothesis of the mind's judging by the various divergency of rays may be of use in determining the apparent place of an object, it will be necessary to premise some few things which are already well known to those who have any skill in dioptrics.

34. *First,* any radiating point is then distinctly seen when the rays proceeding from it are, by the refractive power of the crystalline, accurately reunited in the retina or fund of the eye. But if they are reunited either before they arrive at the retina, or after they have passed it, then there is confused vision.

35. *Secondly,* suppose, in the adjacent figures, *NP* represent an eye duly framed and retaining its natural figure. In Fig. 1, the rays falling nearly parallel on the eye are by the crystalline *AB* refracted, so as their focus, or point of union *F,* falls exactly on the retina. But if the rays fall sensibly diverging on the eye, as in Fig. 2, then their focus falls beyond the retina; or, if the rays are made to converge by the lens *QS* before they come at the eye, as in Fig. 3, their focus *F* will fall before the retina. In which two last cases it is evident, from the foregoing section, that the appearance of the point *Z* is confused. And by how much the greater is the convergency or divergency of the rays falling on the pupil, by so much the farther will the point of their reunion be from the retina, either before or behind it, and consequently the point *Z* will appear by so much the more confused. And this, by the bye, may show us the difference between confused and faint vision. Confused vision is when the rays proceeding from each distinct point of the object are not accurately re-collected in one corresponding

point on the retina, but take up some space thereon—so that
rays from different points become mixed and confused together. This is opposed to a distinct vision, and attends near
objects. Faint vision is when, by reason of the distance of the
object or grossness of the interjacent medium, few rays arrive
from the object to the eye. This is opposed to vigorous or
clear vision, and attends remote objects. But to return.

36. The eye, or (to speak truly) the mind, perceiving only
the confusion itself without ever considering the cause from
which it proceeds, constantly annexes the same degree of distance to the same degree of confusion. Whether that confu-

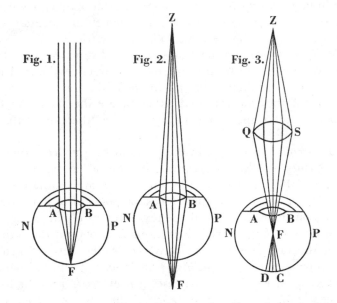

sion be occasioned by converging or by diverging rays it matters not. Whence it follows that the eye, viewing the object Z
through the glass QS (which by refraction causes the rays ZQ,
ZS, etc., to converge), should judge it to be at such a nearness,
at which, if it were placed, it would radiate on the eye, with
rays diverging to that degree as would produce the same confusion which is now produced by converging rays, i.e., would
cover a portion of the retina equal to DC (vide Fig. 3 supra).

But then this must be understood (to use Dr. Barrow's phrase) *seclusis praenotionibus et praejudiciis,* in case we abstract from all other circumstances of vision, such as the figure, size, faintness, etc. of the visible objects—all which do ordinarily concur to form our idea of distance, the mind having, by frequent experience, observed their several sorts or degrees to be connected with various distances.

37. It plainly follows from what has been said that a person perfectly purblind (i.e., that could not see an object distinctly but when placed close to his eye) would not make the same wrong judgment that others do in the forementioned case.[30] For, to him greater confusions constantly suggesting greater distances, he must, as he recedes from the glass and the object grows more confused, judge it to be at a farther distance; contrary to what they do who have had the perception of the objects growing more confused connected with the idea of approach.

38. Hence also it appears there may be good use of computation, by lines and angles, in optics;[31] not that the mind judges of distance immediately by them, but because it judges by somewhat which is connected with them, and to the determination whereof they may be subservient. Thus, the mind judging of the distance of an object by the confusedness of its appearance, and this confusedness being greater or lesser to the naked eye according as the object is seen by rays more or less diverging, it follows that a man may make use of the divergency of the rays in computing the apparent distance, though not for its own sake, yet on account of the confusion with which it is connected. But so it is, the confusion itself is entirely neglected by mathematicians as having no necessary relation with distance, such as the greater or lesser angles of divergency are conceived to have. And these (especially for that they fall under mathematical computation) are alone regarded in determining the apparent places of objects, as though they were the sole and immediate cause of the judg-

[30] [Cf. *Philosophical Commentaries,* sec. 170: "In the Barrovian Case purblind would judge aright."]
[31] [Cf. sec. 78; also *Visual Language,* sec. 31.]

ments the mind makes of distance. Whereas, in truth, they should not at all be regarded in themselves, or any otherwise than as they are supposed to be the cause of confused vision.

39. The not considering of this has been a fundamental and perplexing oversight. For proof whereof we need go no farther than the case before us. It having been observed that the most diverging rays brought into the mind the idea of nearest distance, and that still as the divergency decreased the distance increased, and it being thought the connection between the various degrees of divergency and distance was immediate—this naturally leads one to conclude, from an ill-grounded analogy, that converging rays shall make an object appear at an immense distance, and that, as the convergency increases, the distance (if it were possible) should do so likewise. That this was the cause of Dr. Barrow's mistake is evident from his own words which we have quoted. Whereas had the learned doctor observed that diverging and converging rays, how opposite soever they may seem, do nevertheless agree in producing the same effect, to wit, confusedness of vision, greater degrees whereof are produced differently either as the divergency or convergency of the rays increases; and that it is by this effort, which is the same in both, that either the divergency or convergency is perceived by the eye—I say, had he but considered this, it it certain he would have made a quite contrary judgment, and rightly concluded that those rays which fall on the eye with greater degrees of convergency should make the object from whence they proceed appear by so much the nearer. But it is plain it was impossible for any man to attain to a right notion of this matter so long as he had regard only to lines and angles, and did not apprehend the true nature of vision and how far it was of mathematical consideration.

40. Before we dismiss this subject, it is fit we take notice of a query relating thereto proposed by the ingenious Mr. Molyneux in his *Treatise of Dioptrics* [32] where, speaking of the difficulty we have been explaining, he has these words: "And so he (i.e., Dr. Barrow) leaves this difficulty to the solution of others, which I (after so great an example) shall do likewise;

[32] Par. I, prop. 31, sec. 9.

but with the resolution of the same admirable author of not quitting the evident doctrine which we have before laid down for determining the *locus objecti* on account of being pressed by one difficulty which seems inexplicable till a more intimate knowledge of the visive faculty be obtained by mortals. In the meantime I propose it to the consideration of the ingenious whether the *locus apparens* of an object placed as in this ninth section be not as much before the eye as the distinct base is behind the eye?" To which query we may venture to answer in the negative. For, in the present case, the rule for determining the distance of the distinct base or respective focus from the glass is this: *As the difference between the distance of the object and focus is to the focus or focal length, so the distance of the object from the glass is to the distance of the respective focus or distinct base from the glass.*[33] Let us now suppose the object to be placed at the distance of the focal length, and one-half of the focal length from the glass, and the eye close to the glass. Hence it will follow, by the rule, that the distance of the distinct base behind the eye is double the true distance of the object before the eye. If, therefore, Mr. Molyneux's conjecture held good, it would follow that the eye should see the object twice as far off as it really is, and in other cases at three or four times its due distance, or more. But this manifestly contradicts experience, the object never appearing, at farthest, beyond its due distance. Whatever, therefore, is built on this supposition (*vide* Corol. I, Prop. 57, *ibid.*) comes to the ground along with it.

41. From what has been premised, it is a manifest consequence that a man born blind, being made to see, would at first have no idea of distance by sight: the sun and stars, the remotest objects as well as the nearer, would all seem to be in his eye, or rather in his mind. The objects intromitted by sight would seem to him (as in truth they are) no other than a new set of thoughts or sensations, each whereof is as near to him as the perceptions of pain or pleasure, or the most inward passions of his soul. For our judging objects perceived by sight to be at any distance, or without the mind, is (*vide*

[33] Molyneux, *Dioptrics,* Par. I, prop. 5.

sec. 28) entirely the effect of experience, which one in those circumstances could not yet have attained to.

42. It is indeed otherwise upon the common supposition that men judge of distance by the angle of the optic axes, just as one in the dark, or a blind man by the angle comprehended by two sticks, one whereof he held in each hand.[34] For, if this were true, it would follow that one blind from his birth, being made to see, should stand in need of no new experience in order to perceive distance by sight. But that this is false has, I think, been sufficiently demonstrated.

43. And perhaps, upon a strict inquiry, we shall not find that even those who from their birth have grown up in a continued habit of seeing are irrecoverably prejudiced on the other side, to wit, in thinking what they see to be at a distance from them. For at this time it seems agreed on all hands, by those who have had any thoughts of that matter, that colors, which are the proper and immediate object of sight, are not without the mind. But then, it will be said, by sight we have also the ideas of extension, and figure, and motion; all which may well be thought without and at some distance from the mind, though color should not. In answer to this, I appeal to any man's experience whether the visible extension of any object does not appear as near to him as the color of that object; nay, whether they do not both seem to be in the very same place. Is not the extension we see colored, and is it possible for us, so much as in thought, to separate and abstract color from extension? Now, where the extension is, there surely is the figure, and there the motion too. I speak of those which are perceived by sight.

44. But for a fuller explication of this point, and to show that the immediate objects of sight are not so much as the ideas or resemblances [35] of things placed at a distance, it is requisite that we look nearer into the matter, and carefully observe what is meant in common discourse when one says that which he sees is at a distance from him. Suppose, for ex-

34 [Descartes' device. Cf. Appendix; Descartes' *Dioptrics,* Bk. VI; Malebranche's *The Search,* Bk. I, chap. ix, sec. 3.]

35 [Cf. *Alciphron,* Dial. IV, sec. 9.]

ample, that looking at the moon I should say it were fifty or sixty semidiameters of the earth distant from me. Let us see what moon this is spoken of. It is plain it cannot be the visible moon, or anything like the visible moon, or that which I see— which is only a round luminous plane, of about thirty visible points in diameter. For in case I am carried from the place where I stand directly toward the moon, it is manifest the object varies still as I go on; and, by the time that I am advanced fifty or sixty semidiameters of the earth, I shall be so far from being near a small, round, luminous flat that I shall perceive nothing like it, this object having long since disappeared, and, if I would recover it, it must be by going back to the earth from whence I set out. Again, suppose I perceive by sight the faint and obscure idea of something, which I doubt whether it be a man or a tree or a tower, but judge it to be at the distance of about a mile. It is plain I cannot mean that what I see is a mile off, or that it is the image or likeness of anything which is a mile off; since that every step I take toward it the appearance alters, and from being obscure, small, and faint, grows clear, large, and vigorous. And when I come to the mile's end, that which I saw first is quite lost, neither do I find anything in the likeness of it.

45. In these and the like instances, the truth of the matter, I find, stands thus: Having of a long time experienced certain ideas perceivable by touch—as distance, tangible figure, and solidity—to have been connected with certain ideas of sight, I do, upon perceiving these ideas of sight, forthwith conclude what tangible ideas are, by the wonted ordinary course of nature, like to follow. Looking at an object, I perceive a certain visible figure and color, with some degree of faintness and other circumstances, which, from what I have formerly observed, determine me to think that if I advance forward so many paces or miles I shall be affected with such and such ideas of touch. So that, in truth and strictness of speech, I neither see distance itself, nor anything that I take to be at a distance. I say neither distance nor things placed at a distance themselves, or their ideas, truly perceived by sight. This I am persuaded of, as to what concerns myself. And I believe

whoever will look narrowly into his own thoughts, and examine what he means by saying he sees this or that thing at a distance, will agree with me that what he sees only suggests to his understanding that, after having passed a certain distance, to be measured by the motion of his body, which is perceivable by touch, he shall come to perceive such and such tangible ideas, which have been usually connected with such and such visible ideas. But that one might be deceived by these suggestions of sense, and that there is no necessary connection between visible and tangible ideas suggested by them, we need go no farther than the next looking glass or picture to be convinced.[36] Note that, when I speak of tangible ideas, I take the word "idea" for any immediate object of sense, or understanding—in which large signification it is commonly used by the moderns.

46. From what we have shown, it is a manifest consequence that the ideas of space, outness,[37] and things placed at a distance are not, strictly speaking, the object of sight; they are not otherwise perceived by the eye than by the ear. "Sitting in my study I hear a coach drive along the street; I look through the casement and see it; I walk out and enter into it." Thus common speech would incline one to think I heard, saw, and touched the same thing, to wit, the coach. It is nevertheless certain the ideas intromitted by each sense are widely different and distinct from each other; but, having been observed constantly to go together, they are spoken of as one and the same thing. By the variation of the noise I perceive the different distances of the coach and know that it approaches before I look out. Thus by the ear I perceive distance just after the same manner as I do by the eye.

47. I do not, nevertheless, say I hear distance, in like manner as I say that I see it—the ideas perceived by hearing not

[36] [Cf. *Alciphron*, Dial. IV, sec. 12.]

[37] [A. A. Luce (*Berkeley and Malebranche* [Oxford, 1934], p. 46), points out that the Oxford Dictionary gives no instance of the use of this word before Berkeley's *Essay*. Cf. Malebranche's *The Search*, p. 112: ". . . there are outnesses . . . in the intelligible world. . . ."]

being so apt to be confounded with the ideas of touch as those of sight are. So likewise a man is easily convinced that bodies and external things are not properly the object of hearing, but only sounds, by the mediation whereof the idea of this or that body, or distance, is suggested to his thoughts. But then one is with more difficulty brought to discern the difference there is betwixt the ideas of sight and touch, though it be certain a man no more sees and feels the same thing than he hears and feels the same thing.

48. One reason of which seems to be this. It is thought a great absurdity to imagine that one and the same thing should have any more than one extension and one figure. But the extension and figure of a body being let into the mind two ways, and that indifferently either by sight or touch, it seems to follow that we see the same extension and the same figure which we feel.

49. But if we take a close and accurate view of things,[38] it must be acknowledged that we never see and feel one and the same object. That which is seen is one thing, and that which is felt is another. If the visible figure and extension be not the same with the tangible figure and extension, we are not to infer that one and the same thing has divers extensions. The true consequence is that the objects of sight and touch are two distinct things. It may perhaps require some thought rightly to conceive this distinction. And the difficulty seems not a little increased because the combination of visible ideas has constantly the same name as the combination of tangible ideas wherewith it is connected—which does of necessity arise from the use and end of language.

50. In order, therefore, to treat accurately and unconfusedly of vision, we must bear in mind that there are two sorts of objects apprehended by the eye—the one primarily and immediately, the other secondarily and by intervention of the former. Those of the first sort neither are nor appear to be without the mind, or at any distance off. They may, indeed

38 [View of things—I, II: view of the matter.]

grow greater or smaller, more confused, or more clear, or more faint. But they do not, cannot approach or recede [39] from us. Whenever we say an object is at a distance, whenever we say it draws near or goes farther off, we must always mean it of the latter sort, which properly belong to the touch and are not so truly perceived as suggested by the eye in like manner as thoughts by the ear.

51. No sooner do we hear the words of a familiar language pronounced in our ears but the ideas corresponding thereto present themselves to our minds; in the very same instant the sound and the meaning enter the understanding; so closely are they united that it is not in our power to keep out the one except we exclude the other also. We even act in all respects as if we heard the very thoughts themselves. So likewise the secondary objects, or those which are only suggested by sight, do often more strongly affect us, and are more regarded, than the proper objects of that sense; along with which they enter into the mind, and with which they have a far more strict connection than ideas have with words. Hence it is we find it so difficult to discriminate between the immediate and mediate objects of sight, and are so prone to attribute to the former what belongs only to the latter. They are, as it were, most closely twisted, blended, and incorporated together. And the prejudice is confirmed and riveted in our thoughts by a long tract of time, by the use of language, and want of reflection. However, I believe [40] anyone that shall attentively consider what we have already said, and shall say upon this subject before we have done (especially if he pursue it in his own thoughts), may be able to deliver himself from that prejudice. Sure I am, it is worth some attention to whoever would understand the true nature of vision.[41]

39 [Cannot approach or recede—I, II: cannot approach, or even seem to approach, or recede.]

40 [I believe—I, II: I doubt not, but.]

41 [The conclusion of this analysis of how we see distance, as it is of the analyses of how we see size and situation, is the heterogeneity of the objects of sight and touch—what will later be called, in the synthesis or

52. I have now done with distance, and proceed to show how it is that we perceive by sight the magnitude [42] of objects. It is the opinion of some that we do it by angles, or by angles in conjunction with distance. But neither angles nor distance being perceivable by sight, and the things we see being in truth at no distance from us, it follows that, as we have shown lines and angles not to be the medium the mind makes use of in apprehending the apparent place, so neither are they the medium whereby it apprehends the apparent magnitude of objects.

53. It is well known that the same extension at a near distance shall subtend a greater angle, and at a farther distance a lesser angle. And by this principle (we are told) the mind estimates the magnitude of an object, comparing the angle under which it is seen with its distance, and thence inferring the magnitude thereof.[43] What inclines men to this mistake (beside the humor of making one see by geometry) is that the same perceptions or ideas which suggest distance do also suggest magnitude. But if we examine it, we shall find they suggest the latter as immediately as the former. I say they do not first suggest distance and then leave it to the judgment to use that as a medium whereby to collect the magnitude; but they have as close and immediate a connection with the magnitude

---

theory of vision, the "main part and pillar" of the theory. Cf. *Essay*, sec. 127; *Visual Language*, sec. 41; *Alciphron*, Dial. IV, sec. 7. This heterogeneity now suggests the corresponding heterogeneity of the words and referents of language, and thus the conclusion of the whole analysis—what will later be called, in the synthesis or theory, the principle of visual language. Cf. *Essay*, sec. 147; *Visual Language*, sec. 38; *Alciphron*, Dial. IV, sec. 7.]

42 [How we tell by sight the size of objects is analyzed in secs. 52-87. Cf. *Visual Language*, secs. 53-61.]

43 [Cf. Molyneux's *New Dioptrics*, Part I, prop. 28; Hermann von Helmholtz' "Handbook" (*Treatise on Physiological Optics*), translated from the 3rd German edn. by James P. Southall (Rochester: The Optical Society of America, 1925), III (*The Perceptions of Vision*), 282, 297. (The 1st German edn.; entitled *Handbuch der physiologischen Optik,* appeared at Hamburg and Leipzig, 1856.)]

as with the distance, and suggest magnitude as independently of distance as they do distance independently of magnitude. All which will be evident to whoever considers what has been already said and what follows.

54. It has been shown there are two sorts of objects apprehended by sight, each whereof has its distinct magnitude or extension—the one, properly tangible, i.e., to be perceived and measured by touch, and not immediately falling under the sense of seeing; the other, properly and immediately visible, by mediation of which the former is brought in view. Each of these magnitudes are greater or lesser, according as they contain in them more or fewer points, they being made up of points or minimums. For, whatever may be said of extension in abstract, it is certain sensible extension is not infinitely divisible. There is a *minimum tangibile,* and a *minimum visibile,* beyond which sense cannot perceive. This everyone's experience will inform him.

55. The magnitude of the object which exists without the mind, and is at a distance, continues always invariably the same; but the visible object still changing as you approach to or recede from the tangible object, it has no fixed and determinate greatness. Whenever, therefore, we speak of the magnitude of anything, for instance a tree or a house, we must mean the tangible magnitude; otherwise there can be nothing steady and free from ambiguity spoken of it. But though the tangible and visible magnitude do in truth belong to two distinct objects, I shall nevertheless (especially since those objects are called by the same name and are observed to coexist), to avoid tediousness and singularity of speech, sometimes speak of them as belonging to one and the same thing.

56. Now, in order to discover by what means the magnitude of tangible objects is perceived by sight, I need only reflect on what passes in my own mind, and observe what those things be which introduce the ideas of greater or lesser into my thoughts when I look on any object. And these I find to be, *first,* the magnitude or extension of the visible object which, being immediately perceived by sight, is connected with that

other which is tangible and placed at a distance; *secondly,* the confusion or distinctness; and *thirdly,* the vigorousness or faintness of the aforesaid visible appearance. *Caeteris paribus,* by how much the greater or lesser the visible object is, by so much the greater or lesser do I conclude the tangible object to be. But, be the idea immediately perceived by sight never so large, yet, if it be withal confused, I judge the magnitude of the thing to be but small. If it be distinct and clear, I judge it greater. And, if it be faint, I apprehend it to be yet greater. What is here meant by confusion and faintness has been explained in sec. 35.

57. Moreover, the judgments we make of greatness do, in like manner as those of distance, depend on the disposition of the eye;[44] also on the figure, number, and situation of objects,[45] and other circumstances that have been observed to attend great or small tangible magnitudes. Thus, for instance, the very same quantity of visible extension which in the figure of a tower does suggest the idea of great magnitude shall in the figure of a man suggest the idea of much smaller magnitude. That this is owing to the experience we have had of the usual bigness of a tower and a man, no one, I suppose, need be told.

58. It is also evident that confusion or faintness have no more a necessary connection with little or great magnitude than they have with little or great distance. As they suggest the latter, so they suggest the former to our minds. And, by consequence, if it were not for experience we should no more judge a faint or confused appearance to be connected with great or little magnitude than we should that it was connected with great or little distance.

59. Nor will it be found that great or small visible magnitude has any necessary relation to great or small tangible magnitude, so that the one may certainly[46] be inferred from the other. But, before we come to the proof of this, it is fit

[44] [Eye—I: eyes.]
[45] [Number, and situation of objects—I, II: number of intermediate objects.]   [46] [May certainly—I, II: may certainly and infallibly.]

we consider the difference there is between the extension and figure which is the proper object of touch, and that other which is termed visible; and how the former is principally, though not immediately, taken notice of when we look at any object. This has been before mentioned, but we shall here inquire into the cause thereof. We regard the objects that environ us in proportion as they are adapted to benefit or injure our own bodies, and thereby produce in our minds the sensations of pleasure or pain. Now, bodies operating on our organs by an immediate application, and the hurt or advantage [47] arising therefrom depending altogether on the tangible, and not at all on the visible, qualities of any object: This is a plain reason why those should be regarded by us much more than these. And for this end [48] the visive sense seems to have been bestowed on animals, to wit, that, by the perception of visible ideas (which in themselves are not capable of affecting or anywise altering the frame of their bodies), they may be able to foresee [49] (from the experience they have had what tangible ideas are connected with such and such visible ideas) the damage or benefit which is like to ensue upon the application of their own bodies to this or that body which is at a distance. Which foresight, how necessary it is to the preservation of an animal, everyone's experience can inform him. Hence it is that, when we look at an object, the tangible figure and extension thereof are principally attended to; while there is small heed taken of the visible figure and magnitude, which, though more immediately perceived, do less concern us,[50] and are not fitted to produce any alteration in our bodies.

60. That the matter of fact is true will be evident to anyone who considers that a man placed at ten-foot distance is thought as great as if he were placed at the distance only of five feet, which is true, not with relation to the visible, but

[47] [Hurt or advantage—I, II: hurt and advantage.]
[48] [This end—I, II: this end chiefly.]
[49] [Cf. Malebranche's *The Search*, Bk. I, chaps. v, vi, ix, etc.]
[50] [Concern us—I, II: sensibly affect us.]

tangible greatness of the object, the visible magnitude being far greater at one station than it is at the other.

61. Inches, feet, etc., are settled, stated lengths, whereby we measure objects and estimate their magnitude. We say, for example, an object appears to be six inches, or six feet long. Now, that this cannot be meant of visible inches, etc., is evident, because a visible inch is itself no constant determinate magnitude and cannot therefore serve to mark out and determine the magnitude of any other thing. Take an inch marked upon a ruler; view it successively at the distance of half a foot, a foot, a foot and a half, etc., from the eye; at each of which, and at all the intermediate distances, the inch shall have a different visible extension, i.e., there shall be more or fewer points discerned in it. Now, I ask, which of all these various extensions is that stated determinate one that is agreed on for a common measure of other magnitudes? No reason can be assigned why we should pitch on one more than another. And, except there be some invariable determinate extension fixed on to be marked by the word "inch," it is plain it can be used to little purpose; and to say a thing contains this or that number of inches shall imply no more than that it is extended, without bringing any particular idea of that extension into the mind. Farther, an inch and a foot, from different distances, shall both exhibit the same visible magnitude, and yet at the same time you shall say that one seems several times greater than the other. From all which it is manifest that the judgments we make of the magnitude of objects by sight are altogether in reference to their tangible extension. Whenever we say an object is great or small, of this or that determinate measure, I say, it must be meant of the tangible and not the visible extension which, though immediately perceived, is nevertheless little taken notice of.

62. Now, that there is no necessary connection between these two distinct extensions is evident from hence because our eyes might have been framed in such a manner as to be able to see nothing but what were less than the *minimum*

tangibile. In which case it is not impossible we might have perceived all the objects of sight the very same that we do now; but unto those visible appearances there would not be connected those different tangible magnitudes that are now. Which shows the judgments we make of the magnitude of things placed at a distance, from the various greatness of the immediate objects of sight, do not arise from any essential or necessary, but only a customary, tie which has been observed between them.

63. Moreover, it is not only certain that any idea of sight might not have been connected with this or that idea of touch which we now observe to accompany it, but also that the greater visible magnitudes might have been connected with and introduced into our minds lesser tangible magnitudes, and the lesser visible magnitudes greater tangible magnitudes. Nay, that it actually [51] is so, we have daily experience—that object which makes a strong and large appearance not seeming near so great as another the visible magnitude whereof is much less, but more faint,[52] and the appearance upper, or which is the same thing, painted lower on the retina, which faintness and situation suggest both greater magnitude and greater distance.

64. From which, and from secs. 57 and 58, it is manifest that, as we do not perceive the magnitudes of objects immediately by sight, so neither do we perceive them by the mediation of anything which has a necessary connection with them. Those ideas that now suggest to us the various magnitudes of external objects before we touch them might possibly have suggested no such thing; or they might have signified them in a direct contrary manner, so that the very same ideas on the perception whereof we judge an object to be small might as well have served to make us conclude it great; those ideas being in their own nature equally fitted to bring into our minds the idea of small or great, or no size at all, of outward objects, just as the words of any language are in their own

51 [Actually—I, II: often.]
52 [But more faint—I, II: faint.]

nature indifferent to signify this or that thing, or nothing at all.

65. As we see distance, so we see magnitude. And we see both in the same way that we see shame or anger in the looks of a man. Those passions are themselves invisible; they are nevertheless let in by the eye along with colors and alterations of countenance which are the immediate object of vision, and which signify them for no other reason than barely because they have been observed to accompany them. Without which experience we should no more have taken blushing for a sign of shame than of gladness.

66. We are nevertheless exceedingly prone to imagine those things which are perceived only by the mediation of others to be themselves the immediate objects of sight, or at least to have in their own nature a fitness to be suggested by them before ever they had been experienced to coexist with them. From which prejudice everyone perhaps will not find it easy to emancipate himself, by any [but] the clearest convictions of reason. And there are some grounds to think that, if there was one only invariable and universal language in the world, and that men were born with the faculty of speaking it, it would be the opinion of many [53] that the ideas of [54] other men's minds were properly perceived by the ear, or had at least a necessary and inseparable tie with the sounds that were affixed to them. All which seems to arise from want of a due application of our discerning faculty, thereby to discriminate between the ideas that are in our understandings, and consider them apart from each other; which would preserve us from confounding those that are different, and make us see what ideas do, and what do not, include or imply this or that other idea.

67. There is a celebrated phenomenon the solution whereof I shall attempt to give, by the principles that have been laid down, in reference to the manner wherein we apprehend by sight the magnitude of objects. The apparent magnitude

[53] [Many—I, II: some.]
[54] [Ideas of—I, II, III: ideas in.]

of the moon, when placed in the horizon, is much greater than when it is in the meridian, though the angle under which the diameter of the moon is seen be not observed greater in the former case than in the latter; and the horizontal moon does not constantly appear of the same bigness, but at some times seems far greater than at others.

68. Now, in order to explain the reason of the moon's appearing greater than ordinary in the horizon, it must be observed that the particles which compose our atmosphere intercept the rays of light proceeding from any object to the eye; and, by how much the greater is the portion of atmosphere interjacent between the object and the eye, by so much the more are the rays intercepted, and, by consequence, the appearance of the object rendered more faint, every object appearing more vigorous or more faint in proportion as it sends more or fewer rays into the eye. Now, between the eye and the moon when situated in the horizon there lies a far greater quantity of atmosphere than there does when the moon is in the meridian. Whence it comes to pass that the appearance of the horizontal moon is fainter, and therefore, by sec. 56, it should be thought bigger in that situation than in the meridian, or in any other elevation above the horizon.

69. Further, the air being variously impregnated, sometimes more and sometimes less, with vapors and exhalations fitted to retund and intercept the rays of light, it follows that the appearance of the horizontal moon has not always an equal faintness and, by consequence, that luminary, though in the very same situation, is at one time judged greater than at another.

70. That we have here given the true account of the phenomena of the horizontal moon will, I suppose, be further evident to anyone from the following considerations: *First,* it is plain, that which in this case suggests the idea of greater magnitude must be something which is itself perceived; for that which is unperceived cannot suggest to our perception any other thing. *Secondly,* it must be something that does not constantly remain the same but is subject to some change or

variation; since the appearance of the horizontal moon varies, being at one time greater than at another. And yet, *thirdly,* it cannot be [55] the visible figure or magnitude; since that remains the same, or it is rather lesser, by how much the moon is nearer to the horizon. It remains, therefore, that the true cause is that affection or alteration of the visible appearance which proceeds from the greater paucity of rays arriving at the eye, and which I term faintness; since this answers all the forementioned conditions, and I am not conscious of any other perception that does.

71. Add to this that in misty weather it is a common observation that the appearance of the horizontal moon is far larger than usual, which greatly conspires with and strengthens our opinion. Neither would it prove in the least irreconcilable with what we have said if the horizontal moon should chance sometimes to seem enlarged beyond its usual extent, even in more serene weather. For we must not only have regard to the mist which happens to be in the place where we stand; we ought also to take into our thoughts the whole sum of vapors and exhalations which lie betwixt the eye and the moon: all which co-operating to render the appearance of the moon more faint, and thereby increase its magnitude, it may chance to appear greater than it usually does even in the horizontal position, at a time when, though there be no extraordinary fog or haziness just in the place where we stand, yet the air between the eye and the moon, taken altogether, may be loaded with a greater quantity of interspersed vapors and exhalations than at other times.

72. It may be objected that, in consequence of our principles, the interposition of a body in some degree opaque,

[55] [And yet, *thirdly,* it cannot be—I: *Thirdly,* it must not lie in the external circumjacent or intermediate objects but be an affection of the very visible moon itself; since by looking through a tube, when all other objects are excluded from sight, the appearance is as great as ever. And yet, *fourthly,* it cannot be.—II: *Thirdly,* it must not lie in the circumjacent or intermediate objects, such as mountains, houses, fields, etc. because, that when all those objects are excluded from sight, the appearance is as great as ever. And yet, *fourthly,* it cannot be.]

which may intercept a great part of the rays of light, should render the appearance of the moon in the meridian as large as when it is viewed in the horizon. To which I answer, it is not faintness anyhow applied that suggests greater magnitude; there being no necessary, but only an experimental, connection between those two things. It follows that the faintness which enlarges the appearance must be applied in such sort, and with such circumstances, as have been observed to attend the vision of great magnitudes. When from a distance we [56] behold great objects, the particles of the intermediate air and vapors, which are themselves unperceivable, do interrupt the rays of light, and thereby render the appearance less strong and vivid. Now faintness of appearance, caused in this sort, has been experienced to coexist with great magnitude. But when it is caused by the interposition of an opaque sensible body, this circumstance alters the case; so that a faint appearance this way caused does not suggest greater magnitude, because it has not been experienced to coexist with it.

73. Faintness, as well as all other ideas or perceptions which suggest magnitude or distance, does it in the same way that words suggest the notions to which they are annexed. Now, it is known a word pronounced with certain circumstances, or in a certain context with other words, has not always the same import and signification that it has when pronounced in some other circumstances, or different context of words. The very same visible [57] appearance, as to faintness and all other respects, if placed on high, shall not suggest the same magnitude that it would if it were seen at an equal distance on a level with the eye. The reason whereof is that we are rarely accustomed to view objects at a great height; our concerns lie among things situated rather before than above us; and accordingly our eyes are not placed on the top of our heads, but in such a position as is most convenient for us to

---

[56] [Distance we—I: distance (I speak with the vulgar) we.]

[57] [The very same visible . . . explication of it. (i.e., to end of section 73)—I: This well considered may, perhaps, prevent some objections that might otherwise be made against what we have offered as the true explication of the appearance of the horizontal moon.]

see distant objects standing in our way. And, this situation of
them being a circumstance which usually attends the vision
of distant objects, we may from hence account for (what is
commonly observed) an object's appearing of different magnitude, even with respect to its horizontal extension, on the top
of a steeple, for example, a hundred feet high, to one standing
below, from what it would if placed at a hundred feet distance, on a level with his eye. For it has been shown that the
judgment we make on the magnitude of a thing depends not
on the visible appearance only, but also on diverse other circumstances, any one of which being omitted or varied may
suffice to make some alteration in our judgment. Hence, the
circumstance of viewing a distant object in such a situation as
is usual and suits with the ordinary posture of the head and
eyes, being omitted, and instead thereof a different situation
of the object, which requires a different posture of the head,
taking place, it is not to be wondered at if the magnitude be
judged different. But it will be demanded why a high object
should constantly appear less than an equidistant low object
of the same dimensions, for so it is observed to be. It may indeed be granted that the variation of some circumstances may
vary the judgment made on the magnitude of high objects,
which we are less used to look at; but it does not hence appear
why they should be judged less rather than greater. I answer
that, in case the magnitude of distant objects was suggested by
the extent of their visible appearance alone, and thought proportional thereto, it is certain they would then be judged
much less than now they seem to be (*vide* sec. 79). But, several
circumstances concurring to form the judgment we make on
the magnitude of distant objects, by means of which they appear far larger than others whose visible appearance has an
equal or even greater extension, it follows that upon the
change or omission of any of those circumstances which are
wont to attend the vision of distant objects, and so come to
influence the judgments made on their magnitude, they shall
proportionably appear less than otherwise they would. For,
any of those things that caused an object to be thought greater
than in proportion to its visible extension being either

omitted, or applied without the usual circumstances, the judgment depends more entirely on the visible extension, and consequently the object must be judged less. Thus in the present case the situation of the thing seen being different from what it usually is in those objects we have occasion to view, and whose magnitude we observe, it follows that the very same object being a hundred feet high should seem less than if it was a hundred feet off, on (or nearly on) a level with the eye. What has been here set forth seems to me to have no small share in contributing to magnify the appearance of the horizontal moon, and deserves not to be passed over in the explication of it.

74. If we attentively consider the phenomenon before us, we shall find the not discerning between the mediate and immediate objects of sight to be the chief cause of the difficulty that occurs in the explication of it. The magnitude of the visible moon, or that which is the proper and immediate object of vision, is no greater when the moon is in the horizon than when it is in the meridian. How comes it, therefore, to seem greater in one situation than the other? What is it can put this cheat on the understanding? It has no other perception of the moon than what it gets by sight. And that which is seen is of the same extent—I say, the visible appearance has the same, or rather a less, magnitude, when the moon is viewed in the horizontal than when in the meridional position. And yet it is esteemed greater in the former than in the latter. Herein consists the difficulty, which does vanish and admit of a most easy solution, if we consider that as the visible moon is not greater in the horizon than in the meridian, so neither is it thought to be so. It has been already shown that in any act of vision the visible object absolutely, or in itself, is little taken notice of, the mind still carrying its view from that to some tangible ideas which have been observed to be connected with it, and by that means come to be suggested by it. So that when a thing is said to appear great or small, or whatever estimate be made of the magnitude of anything, this is meant not of the visible but of the tangible object. This

duly considered, it will be no hard matter to reconcile the seeming contradiction there is, that the moon should appear of a different bigness, the visible magnitude thereof remaining still the same. For, by sec. 56, the very same visible extension, with a different faintness, shall suggest a different tangible extension. When, therefore, the horizontal moon is said to appear greater than the meridional moon, this must be understood, not of a greater visible extension, but of a greater tangible or real [58] extension which, by reason of the more than ordinary faintness of the visible appearance, is suggested to the mind along with it.

75. Many attempts have been made by learned men to account for this appearance. Gassendus,[59] Descartes,[60] Hobbes,[61] and several others [62] have employed their thoughts on that subject; but how fruitless and unsatisfactory their endeavors have been is sufficiently shown in *The Philosophical Transactions* [63] where you may see their several opinions at large set forth and confuted, not without some surprise at the

[58] [Tangible or real—I, II: tangible.]

[59] [See Appendix to *Essay*, note 4, pp. 100 f.]

[60] [See *Dioptrics*, Bk. VI.]

[61] [See *The English Works of Thomas Hobbes* . . . , 11 vols. (Sir W. Molesworth edn., 1839-1845), I, 462.]

[62] [E.g., Ptolemy, Ibn al-Haitham, Witelo, Roger Bacon, Huygens, *et al.* Helmholtz' *Handbook*, III, 364, asks what he calls "the real question": "Why does the firmament look nearer to us at the zenith than it does around the horizon?" The problem, as old as optics itself, remains very much alive. Cf. Vasco Ronchi's *Optics: The Science of Vision*, p. 120; *Science*, Vol. 130, Sept. 4, 13, 1959; *Science Digest*, Vol. 48, Aug., 1960; and *Scientific American*, Vol. 207, No. 1, July, 1962. In the last article referred to, "The Moon Illusion," by Lloyd Kaufman and Irvin Rock, the authors conclude: "In sum we have demonstrated that the moon illusion depends on the presence of terrain and specifically on the distance effect of the terrain. Eye elevation, color and apparent brightness evidently have nothing to do with the phenomenon. . . . Eighteen hundred years after Ptolemy we have tested his hypothesis and provided evidence that it is correct." For Berkeley's rejection of the Ptolemaic hypothesis, see sec. 77 below.]

[63] *Phil. Trans.* No. 187, p. 314. [In *The Philosophical Transactions*— I, II: by Mr. Molyneux, *vide Phil. Trans.* 187, p. 314— (without footnote).]

gross blunders that ingenious men have been forced into by endeavoring to reconcile this appearance with the ordinary principles of optics. Since the writing of which there has been published in the *Transactions* [64] another paper relating to the same affair by the celebrated Dr. Wallis [65] wherein he attempts [66] to account for that phenomenon which, though it seems not to contain anything new or different from what had been said before by others, I shall nevertheless consider in this place.

76. His opinion, in short, is this: We judge not of the magnitude of an object by the visual angle [67] alone, but by the visual angle [68] in conjunction with the distance. Hence, though the angle remain the same, or even become less, yet if withal the distance seem to have been increased, the object shall appear greater. Now, one way whereby we estimate the distance of anything is by the number and extent of the intermediate objects. When, therefore, the moon is seen in the horizon, the variety of fields, houses, etc., together with the large prospect of the wide extended land or sea that lies between the eye and the utmost limb of the horizon, suggest unto the mind the idea of greater distance, and consequently magnify the appearance. And this, according to Dr. Wallis, is the true account of the extraordinary largeness attributed by the mind to the horizontal moon at a time when the angle subtended by its diameter is not one jot greater than it used to be.

77. With reference to this opinion, not to repeat what has been already said concerning distance, I shall only observe, *first,* that if the prospect of interjacent objects be that which suggests the idea of farther distance, and this idea of farther distance be the cause that brings into the mind the idea of

---

64 *Ibid.,* p. 323.

65 [John Wallis (1616-1703), author of *Arithmetic of Infinites* (Oxford, 1656).]

66 [Attempts—I, II: pretends.]

67 [Visual angle—I, II: optic angle.]

68 *Idem.*

greater magnitude, it should hence follow that if one looked at the horizontal moon from behind a wall, it would appear no bigger than ordinary. For in that case the wall interposing cuts off all that prospect of sea and land, etc., which might otherwise increase the apparent distance, and thereby the apparent magnitude of the moon. Nor will it suffice to say, the memory does even then suggest all that extent of land, etc., which lies within the horizon, which suggestion occasions a sudden judgment of sense that the moon is farther off and larger than usual. For, ask any man who from such a station beholding the horizontal moon shall think her greater than usual, whether he has at that time in his mind any idea of the intermediate objects, or long tract of land that lies between his eye and the extreme edge of the horizon? And whether it be that idea which is the cause of his making the aforementioned judgment? He will, I suppose,[69] reply in the negative, and declare the horizontal moon shall appear greater than the meridional, though he never thinks of all or any of those things that lie between him and it.[70] *Secondly*, it seems impossible by this hypothesis, to account for the moon's appearing, in the very same situation, at one time greater than at another; which, nevertheless, has been shown to be very agreeable to the principles we have laid down, and receives a most easy and natural explication from them.[71] For the further clearing up of this point, it is to be observed, that what we immediately and properly see are only lights and colors in sundry situations and shades, and degrees of faintness and clearness, confusion and distinctness. All which visible objects are only in the mind; nor do they suggest aught external, whether distance or magnitude, otherwise than by habitual

[69] [I suppose—I, II: without doubt.]

[70] [Him and it.—I, II: him and it. And as for the absurdity of any idea introducing into the mind another, while itself is not perceived, this has already fallen under our observation, and is too evident to need any further enlargement on it.]

[71] [Explication from them. For the further clearing up of this point, . . . suggest distance. (i.e., to end of section 77)—I, II: explication from them.]

connection, as words do things. We are also to remark that beside the straining of the eyes, and beside the vivid and faint, the distinct and confused appearances (which, bearing some proportion to lines and angles, have been substituted instead of them in the foregoing part of this treatise), there are other means which suggest both distance and magnitude, particularly the situation of visible points or objects, as upper or lower, the one suggesting a farther distance and greater magnitude, the other a nearer distance and lesser magnitude—all which is an effect only of custom and experience, there being really nothing intermediate in the line of distance between the uppermost and the lowermost, which are both equidistant, or rather at no distance from the eye; as there is also nothing in upper or lower which by necessary connection should suggest greater or lesser magnitude. Now, as these customary experimental means of suggesting distance do likewise suggest magnitude, so they suggest the one as immediately as the other. I say, they do not (*vide* sec. 53) first suggest distance, and then leave the mind from thence to infer or compute magnitude, but suggest magnitude as immediately and directly as they suggest distance.

78. This phenomenon of the horizontal moon is a clear instance of the insufficiency of lines and angles for explaining the way wherein the mind perceives and estimates the magnitude of outward objects. There is, nevertheless, a use of computation by them: in order to determine the apparent magnitude of things, so far as they have a connection with and are proportional to those other ideas or perceptions which are the true and immediate occasions that suggest to the mind the apparent magnitude of things. But this in general may, I think, be observed concerning mathematical computation in optics: that it can never [72] be very precise and exact, since the judgments we make of the magnitude of external things do often depend on several circumstances which are not proportionable to or capable of being defined by lines and angles.

79. From what has been said, we may safely deduce this

[72] [Can never—I, II: can hardly.]

consequence, to wit, that a man born blind, and made to see, would, at first opening of his eyes, make a very different judgment of the magnitude of objects intromitted by them from what others do. He would not consider the ideas of sight with reference to or as having any connection with the ideas of touch. His view of them being entirely terminated within themselves, he cannot otherwise judge them great or small than as they contain a greater or lesser number of visible points. Now, it being certain that any visible point can cover or exclude from view only one other visible point, it follows that whatever object intercepts the view of another has an equal number of visible points with it; and consequently, they shall both be thought by him to have the same magnitude. Hence, it is evident one in those circumstances would judge his thumb, with which he might hide a tower, or hinder its being seen, equal to that tower; or his hand, the interposition whereof might conceal the firmament from his view, equal to the firmament: how great an inequality soever there may, in our apprehensions, seem to be betwixt those two things, because of the customary and close connection that has grown up in our minds between the objects of sight and touch, whereby the very different and distinct ideas of those two senses are so blended and confounded together as to be mistaken for one and the same thing—out of which prejudice we cannot easily extricate ourselves.[73]

80. For better explaining the nature of vision and setting the manner wherein we perceive magnitudes in a due light, I shall proceed to make some observations concerning matters relating thereto, whereof the want of reflection and duly separating between tangible and visible ideas is apt to create in us mistaken and confused notions. And, *first,* I shall observe that the *minimum visibile* is exactly equal in all beings whatsoever that are endowed with the visive faculty.[74] No exquisite for-

[73] [Easily extricate ourselves—I, II: totally extricate ourselves without some labor and striving of thought.]

[74] [Cf. sec. 54. *Minima* are defined (*Philosophical Commentaries,* sec. 70) as "the simplest constituent parts or elements." Cf. Plato, *Theaetetus,* 201: "The letters of the alphabet or elements out of which you and I and

mation of the eye, no peculiar sharpness of sight, can make it less in one creature than in another; for, it not being distinguishable into parts, nor in anywise consisting of them, it must necessarily be the same to all. For, suppose it otherwise, and that the *minimum visibile* of a mite, for instance, be less than the *minimum visibile* of a man; the latter therefore may, by detraction of some part, be made equal to the former. It therefore consists of parts, which is inconsistent with the notion of a *minimum visibile* or point.

81. It will, perhaps, be objected, that the *minimum visibile* of a man does really and in itself contain parts whereby it surpasses that of a mite, though they are not perceivable by the man. To which I answer, the *minimum visibile* having (in like manner as all other the proper and immediate objects of sight) been shown not to have any existence without the mind of him who sees it, it follows there cannot be any part of it that is not actually perceived and therefore visible. Now, for any object to contain several distinct visible parts, and at the same time to be a *minimum visibile,* is a manifest contradiction.

82. Of these visible points we see at all times an equal number. It is every whit as great when our view is contracted and bounded by near objects as when it is extended to larger and remoter. For, it being impossible that one *minimum visibile* should obscure or keep out of sight more than one other, it is a plain consequence that, when my view is on all sides bounded by the walls of my study, I see just as many visible points as I could in case that, by the removal of the study

---

all other things are compounded. . . ." This section is criticized by Archbishop King (Cf. Appendix to *Essay*, note 1, p. 98.) and by "Anti-Berkeley" in a letter to *Gentleman's Magazine*, XXII, 12 (Jan., 1752). The latter states: "There are animals whose whole bodies are far less than the *minimum visibile* of a man. Doubtless these animals have eyes, and, if their *minimum visibile* were equal to that of a man, it would follow that they cannot perceive anything but what is much larger than their whole body; and therefore their own bodies must be invisible to them, because we know they are so to men, whose *minimum visibile* is asserted by his lordship to be equal to theirs." Cf. Appendix to *Essay*.]

walls and all other obstructions, I had a full prospect of the circumjacent fields, mountains, sea, and open firmament. For, so long as I am shut up within the walls, by their interposition every point of the external objects is covered from my view. But each point that is seen being able to cover or exclude from sight one only other corresponding point, it follows that, while my sight is confined to those narrow walls, I see as many points, or *minima visibilia,* as I should were those walls away, by looking on all the external objects whose prospect is intercepted by them. Whenever, therefore, we are said to have a greater prospect at one time than another, this must be understood with relation not to the proper and immediate, but the secondary and mediate objects of vision—which, as has been shown, properly belong to the touch.

83. The visive faculty, considered with reference to its immediate objects, may be found to labor of two defects. *First,* in respect of the extent or number of visible points that are at once perceivable by it, which is narrow and limited to a certain degree. It can take in at one view but a certain determinate number of *minima visibilia,* beyond which it cannot extend its prospect. *Secondly,* our sight is defective in that its view is not only narrow, but also for the most part confused. Of those things that we take in at one prospect, we can see but a few at once clearly and unconfusedly; and the more we fix our sight on any one object, by so much the darker and more indistinct shall the rest appear.

84. Corresponding to these two defects of sight, we may imagine as many perfections, to wit, *first,* that of comprehending in one view a greater number of visible points; *secondly,* of being able to view them all equally and at once, with the utmost clearness and distinction. That those perfections are not actually in some intelligences of a different order and capacity from ours, it is impossible for us to know.

85. In neither of those two ways do microscopes contribute to the improvement of sight. For, when we look through a microscope, we neither see more visible points nor are the collateral points more distinct than when we look with the naked

eye at objects placed in a due distance. A microscope brings us, as it were, into a new world. It presents us with a new scene of visible objects, quite different from what we behold with the naked eye. But herein consists the most remarkable difference, to wit, that whereas the objects perceived by the eye alone have a certain connection with tangible objects, whereby we are taught to foresee what will ensue upon the approach or application of distant objects to the parts of our own body, which much conduces to its preservation, there is not the like connection between things tangible and those visible objects that are perceived by help of a fine microscope.

86. Hence, it is evident that, were our eyes turned into the nature of microscopes, we should not be much benefited by the change. We should be deprived of the forementioned advantage we at present receive by the visive faculty, and have left us only the empty amusement of seeing, without any other benefit arising from it. But, in that case, it will perhaps be said, our sight would be endued with a far greater sharpness and penetration than it now has. But it is certain,[75] from what we have already shown, that the *minimum visibile* is never greater or lesser, but in all cases constantly the same. And in the case of microscopical eyes I see only this difference, to wit, that upon the ceasing of a certain observable connection betwixt the divers perceptions of sight and touch, which before enabled us to regulate our actions by the eye, it would now be rendered utterly unserviceable to that purpose.[76]

87. Upon the whole, it seems that if we consider the use and end of sight, together with the present state and circumstances of our being, we shall not find any great cause to complain of any defect or imperfection in it, or easily conceive how it could be mended. With such admirable wisdom is that faculty contrived, both for the pleasure and convenience of life.

[75] [But it is certain—I, II, III: But I would fain know wherein consists that sharpness which is esteemed so great an excellency of sight. It is certain.]

[76] [Purpose.—I, II: purpose. Which whether it be a desirable perfection, or no, I leave it to anyone to determine.]

88. Having finished what I intended to say concerning the distance and magnitude of objects, I come now to treat of the manner wherein the mind perceives by sight their situation.[77] Among the discoveries of the last age it is reputed none of the least that the manner of vision has been more clearly explained than ever it had been before. There is at this day no one ignorant that the pictures of external objects are painted on the retina or fund of the eye; that we can see nothing which is not so painted; and that, according as the picture is more distinct or confused, so also is the perception we have of the object. But then, in this explication of vision, there occurs one mighty difficulty. The objects are painted in an inverted order on the bottom of the eye, the upper part of any object being painted on the lower part of the eye, and the lower part of the object on the upper part of the eye; and so also as to right and left. Since therefore the pictures are thus inverted, it is demanded how it comes to pass that we see the objects erect and in their natural posture?

89. In answer to this difficulty we are told that the mind, perceiving an impulse of a ray of light on the upper part of the eye, considers this ray as coming in a direct line from the lower part of the object; and in like manner, tracing the ray that strikes on the lower part of the eye, it is directed to the upper part of the object. Thus, in the adjacent figure, C, the lower point of the object ABC, is projected on c, the upper

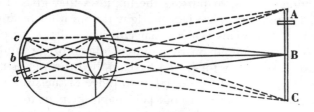

part of the eye. So likewise, the highest point A is projected on a, the lowest part of the eye; which makes the representation cba inverted. But the mind—considering the stroke that is

made on *c* as coming in the straight line *Cc* from the lower
end of the object; and the stroke or impulse on *a* as coming in
the line *Aa* from the upper end of the object—is directed to
make a right judgment of the situation of the object *ABC*,
notwithstanding the picture of it is inverted. This is illustrated by conceiving a blind man who, holding in his hands
two sticks that cross each other, does with them touch the
extremities of an object, placed in a perpendicular situation.
It is certain this man will judge that to be the upper part of
the object which he touches with the stick held in the undermost hand, and that to be the lower part of the object which
he touches with the stick in his uppermost hand. This is the
common explication of the erect appearance of objects, which
is generally received and acquiesced in, being (as Mr. Molyneux tells us),[78] "allowed by all men as satisfactory."

90. But this account [79] to me does not seem in any degree
true. Did I perceive those impulses, decussations and direc-
tions of the rays of light, in like manner as has been set forth,
then, indeed, it would not [80] be altogether void of probability.
And there might be some pretense for the comparison of the
blind man and his cross sticks. But the case is far otherwise. I
know very well that I perceive no such thing. And, of consequence, I cannot thereby make an estimate of the situation of
objects. I appeal to anyone's experience, whether he be conscious to himself that he thinks on the intersection made by
the radius pencils, or pursues the impulses they give in right
lines, whenever he perceives by sight the position of any object. To me it seems evident that crossing and tracing of the
rays is never thought on by children, idiots, or, in truth, by
any other, save only those who have applied themselves to the
study of optics. And for the mind to judge of the situation of
objects by those things without perceiving them, or to perceive
them without knowing it, is equally [81] beyond my comprehen-

78 *Dioptrics*, Par. II, c. 7, p. 289.
79 [But this account—I, II: But how reasonable and satisfactory soever
this account may be thought by others, to me certainly it.]
80 [It would not—I, II, III: it would not at first view.]
81 [Is equally—I, II: take which you please, 'tis perfectly.]

sion. Add to this that explaining the manner of vision by the example of cross sticks, and hunting for the object along the axes of the radius pencils, supposes the proper objects of sight to be perceived at a distance from us, contrary to what has been demonstrated.[82]

91. It remains, therefore, that we look for some other explication of this difficulty. And I believe it not impossible to find one, provided we examine it to the bottom, and carefully distinguish between the ideas of sight and touch; which cannot be too oft inculcated in treating of vision. But more especially throughout the consideration of this affair, we ought to carry that distinction in our thoughts; for that from want of a right understanding thereof, the difficulty of explaining erect vision seems chiefly to arise.

92. In order to disentangle our minds from whatever prejudices we may entertain with relation to the subject in hand, nothing seems more apposite than the taking into our thoughts the case of one born blind, and afterward, when grown up, made to see. And—though perhaps it may not be an easy task [83] to divest ourselves entirely of the experience received from sight so as to be able to put our thoughts exactly in the posture of such a one's—we must, nevertheless, as far as possible, endeavor to frame true conceptions of what might reasonably be supposed to pass in his mind.

93. It is certain that a man actually blind, and who had continued so from his birth, would by the sense of feeling, attain to have ideas of upper and lower. By the motion of his hand, he might discern the situation of any tangible object placed within his reach. That part on which he felt himself supported, or toward which he perceived his body to gravitate, he would term "lower," and the contrary to this "upper," and accordingly denominate whatsoever objects he touched.

[82] [Been demonstrated.—I, II: been demonstrated. We may therefore venture to pronounce this opinion concerning the way wherein the mind perceives the erect appearance of objects to be of a piece with those other tenets of writers in optics, which in the foregoing parts of this treatise we have had occasion to examine and refute.]

[83] [An easy task—I, II: a task altogether easy and familiar to us.]

94. But then, whatever judgments he makes concerning the situation of objects are confined to those only that are perceivable by touch. All those things that are intangible, and of a spiritual nature—his thoughts and desires, his passions, and in general all the modifications of his soul—to these he would never apply the terms "upper" and "lower," except only in a metaphorical sense. He may perhaps, by way of allusion, speak of "high" or "low" thoughts: but those terms, in their proper signification, would never be applied to anything that was not conceived to exist without the mind. For, a man born blind, and remaining in the same state, could mean nothing else by the words "higher" and "lower" than a greater or lesser distance from the earth; which distance he would measure by the motion or application of his hand, or some other part of his body. It is, therefore, evident that all those things which, in respect of each other, would by him be thought higher or lower must be such as were conceived to exist without his mind, in the ambient space.

95. Whence it plainly follows that such a one, if we suppose him made to see, would not at first sight think that anything he saw was high or low, erect or inverted. For, it has been already demonstrated, in sec. 41, that he would not think the things he perceived by sight to be at any distance from him, or without his mind. The objects to which he had hitherto been used to apply the terms "up" and "down," "high" and "low," were such only as affected or were some way perceived by his touch. But the proper objects of vision make a new set of ideas, perfectly distinct and different from the former, and which can in no sort make themselves perceived by touch. There is, therefore, nothing at all that could induce him to think those terms applicable to them. Nor would he ever think it till such time as he had observed their connection with tangible objects, and the same prejudice began to insinuate itself into his understanding which, from their infancy, had grown up in the understandings of other men.

96. To set this matter in a clearer light, I shall make use of an example. Suppose the above-mentioned blind person, by

his touch, perceives a man to stand erect. Let us inquire into the manner of this. By the application of his hand to the several parts of a human body, he had perceived different tangible ideas, which, being collected into sundry complex ones, have distinct names annexed to them. Thus, one combination of a certain tangible figure, bulk, and consistency of parts is called the head; another the hand; a third the foot, and so of the rest—all which complex ideas could, in his understanding, be made up only of ideas perceivable by touch. He had also, by his touch, obtained an idea of earth or ground, toward which he perceives the parts of his body to have a natural tendency. Now—by "erect" nothing more being meant than that perpendicular position of a man wherein his feet are nearest to the earth—if the blind person, by moving his hand over the parts of the man who stands before him perceives the tangible ideas that compose the head to be farthest from, and those that compose the feet to be nearest to, that other combination of tangible ideas which he calls "earth," he will denominate that man "erect." But, if we suppose him on a sudden to receive his sight, and that he behold a man standing before him, it is evident in that case he would neither judge the man he sees to be erect nor inverted; for he, never having known those terms applied to any other save tangible things, or which existed in the space without him, and what he sees neither being tangible, nor perceived as existing without, he could not know that, in propriety of language, they were applicable to it.

97. Afterward when, upon turning his head or eyes up and down to the right and left, he shall observe the visible objects to change, and shall also attain to know that they are called by the same names, and connected with the objects perceived by touch; then, indeed, he will come to speak of them and their situation in the same terms that he has been used to apply to tangible things: and those that he perceives by turning up his eyes he will call "upper," and those that by turning down his eyes he will call "lower."

98. And this seems to me the true reason why he should

think those objects uppermost that are painted on the lower part of his eye. For, by turning the eye up they shall be distinctly seen; as likewise those that are painted on the highest part of the eye shall be distinctly seen by turning the eye down, and are for that reason esteemed lowest. For we have shown that to the immediate objects of sight, considered in themselves, he would not attribute the terms "high" and "low." It must therefore be on account of some circumstances which are observed to attend them. And these, it is plain, are the actions of turning the eye up and down, which suggest a very obvious reason why the mind should denominate the objects of sight accordingly "high" or "low." And without this motion of the eye—this turning it up and down in order to discern different objects—doubtless "erect," "inverse," and other the like terms relating to the position of tangible objects, would never have been transferred, or in any degree apprehended to belong to the ideas of sight, the mere act of seeing including nothing in it to that purpose; whereas the different situations of the eye naturally direct the mind to make a suitable judgment of the situation of objects intromitted by it.

99. Further, when he has by experience learned the connection there is between the several ideas of sight and touch he will be able, by the perception he has of the situation of visible things in respect of one another, to make a sudden and true estimate of the situation of outward, tangible things corresponding to them. And thus it is he shall perceive by sight the situation of external objects, which do not properly fall under that sense.

100. I know we are very prone to think that if just made to see we should judge of the situation of visible things as we do now. But we are also as prone to think that, at first sight, we should in the same way apprehend the distance and magnitude of objects as we do now; which has been shown to be a false and groundless persuasion. And for the like reasons, the same censure may be passed on the positive assurance that most men, before they have thought sufficiently of the matter,

might have of their being able to determine by the eye, at first view, whether objects were erect or inverse.

101. It will perhaps be objected to our opinion, that a man, for instance, being thought erect when his feet are next the earth, and inverted when his head is next the earth, it hence follows that, by the mere act of vision, without any experience or altering the situation of the eye, we should have determined whether he were erect or inverted. For both the earth itself, and the limbs of the man who stands thereon, being equally perceived by sight, one cannot choose seeing what part of the man is nearest the earth, and what part farthest from it, i.e., whether he be erect or inverted.

102. To which I answer, the ideas which constitute the tangible earth and man are entirely different from those which constitute the visible earth and man. Nor was it possible, by virtue of the visive faculty alone, without superadding any experience of touch or altering the position of the eye, ever to have known, or so much as suspected, there had been any relation or connection between them. Hence, a man at first view would not denominate anything he saw "earth," or "head," or "foot": and consequently, he could not tell by the mere act of vision whether the head or feet were nearest the earth. Nor, indeed, would we have thereby any thought of earth or man, erect or inverse, at all—which will be made yet more evident, if we nicely observe and make a particular comparison between the ideas of both senses.

103. That which I see is only variety of light and colors. That which I feel is hard or soft, hot or cold, rough or smooth. What similitude, what connection, have those ideas with these? Or, how is it possible that anyone should see reason to give one and the same name to combinations of ideas so very different before he had experienced their coexistence? We do not find there is any necessary connection betwixt this or that tangible quality, and any color whatsoever. And we may sometimes perceive colors where there is nothing to be felt. All which makes it manifest that no man at first receiving of his sight would know there was any agreement between this or

that particular object of his sight and any object of touch he had been already acquainted with. The colors therefore of the head would to him no more suggest the idea of head than they would the idea of foot.

104. Further, we have at large shown (*vide* secs. 63 and 64) there is no discoverable necessary connection between any given visible magnitude and any one particular tangible magnitude; but that it is entirely the result of custom and experience and depends on foreign and accidental circumstances that we can, by the perception of visible extension, inform ourselves what may be the extension of any tangible object connected with it. Hence, it is certain that neither the visible magnitude of head or foot would bring along with them into the mind, at first opening of the eyes, the respective tangible magnitudes of those parts.

105. By the foregoing section it is plain the visible figure of any part of the body has no necessary connection with the tangible figure thereof so as at first sight to suggest it to the mind. For, figure is the termination of magnitude. Whence it follows that no visible magnitude having in its own nature an aptness to suggest any one particular tangible magnitude, so neither can any visible figure be inseparably connected with its corresponding tangible figure, so as of itself, and in a way prior to experience, it might suggest it to the understanding. This will be further evident if we consider that what seems smooth and round to the touch may to sight, if viewed through a microscope, seem quite otherwise.

106. From all which, laid together and duly considered, we may clearly deduce this inference: In the first act of vision, no idea entering by the eye would have a perceivable connection with the ideas to which the names "earth," "man," "head," "foot," etc., were annexed in the understanding of a person blind from his birth, so as in any sort to introduce them into his mind, or make themselves be called by the same names, and reputed the same things with them as afterward they come to be.

107. There does, nevertheless, remain one difficulty, which

perhaps [84] may seem to press hard on our opinion, and deserves not to be passed over. For, though it be granted that neither the color, size, nor figure of the visible feet have any necessary connection with the ideas that compose the tangible feet so as to bring them at first sight into my mind, or make me in danger of confounding them, before I had been used to and for some time experienced their connection; yet thus much seems undeniable, namely, that the number of the visible feet being the same with that of the tangible feet, I may from hence, without any experience of sight, reasonably conclude that they represent or are connected with the feet rather than the head. I say, it seems the idea of two visible feet will sooner suggest to the mind the idea of two tangible feet than of one head, so that the blind man, upon first reception of the visive faculty, might know which were the feet, or two, and which the head, or one.

108. In order to get clear of this seeming difficulty we need only observe that diversity of visible objects does not necessarily infer diversity of tangible objects corresponding to them. A picture painted with great variety of colors affects the touch in one uniform manner; it is therefore evident that I do not, by any necessary consecution, independent of experience, judge of the number of things tangible from the number of things visible. I should not therefore at first opening my eyes conclude that because I see two I shall feel two. How, therefore, can I, before experience teaches me, know that the visible legs, because two, are connected with the tangible legs; or the visible head, because one, is connected with the tangible head? The truth is, the things I see are so very different and heterogeneous from the things I feel that the perception of the one would never have suggested the other to my thoughts or enabled me to pass the least judgment thereon until I had experienced their connection.

109. But, for a fuller illustration of this matter, it ought to be considered that number (however some [85] may reckon it

84 [Which perhaps—I, II: which to some perhaps.]
85 [E.g., Locke, *Essay*, Bk. II, chap. viii, sec. 17. Cf. Aristotle (*De Anima*

amongst the primary qualities) is nothing fixed and settled, really existing in things themselves. It is entirely the creature of the mind, considering either an idea by itself or any combination of ideas to which it gives one name, and so makes it pass for a unit. According as the mind variously combines its ideas, the unit varies; and as the unit, so the number, which is only a collection of units, also varies. We call a window "one," a chimney "one"; and yet a house, in which there are many windows and many chimneys, has an equal right to be called "one"; and many houses go to the making of one city. In these and the like instances, it is evident the unit constantly relates to the particular drafts the mind makes of its ideas, to which it affixes names, and wherein it includes more or less, as best suits its own ends and purposes. Whatever, therefore, the mind considers as one, that is a unit. Every combination of ideas is considered as one thing by the mind, and in token thereof is marked by one name. Now, this naming and combining together of ideas is perfectly arbitrary, and done by the mind in such sort as experience shows it to be most convenient—without which our ideas had never been collected into such sundry distinct combinations as they now are.

110. Hence it follows that a man born blind, and afterward, when grown up, made to see, would not, in the first act of vision, parcel out the ideas of sight into the same distinct collections that others do who have experienced which do regularly coexist and are proper to be bundled up together under one name. He would not, for example, make into one complex idea and thereby esteem a unit all those particular ideas which constitute the visible head or foot. For there can be no reason assigned why he should do so barely upon his seeing a man stand upright before him. There crowd into his mind the ideas which compose the visible man, in company with all the other ideas of sight perceived at the same time. But all these ideas offered at once to his view he would not distribute into

---

II, 6): "Common sensibles include movement, rest, number, figure, magnitude. . . ."]

sundry distinct combinations, till such time as, by observing the motion of the parts of the man and other experiences, he comes to know which are to be separated and which to be collected together.

111. From what has been premised, it is plain the objects of sight and touch make, if I may so say, two sets of ideas which are widely different from each other. To objects of either kind we indifferently attribute the terms "high" and "low," "right" and "left," and suchlike, denoting the position or situation of things; but then we must well observe that the position of any object is determined with respect only to objects of the same sense. We say any object of touch is "high" or "low," according as it is more or less distant from the tangible earth; and in like manner we denominate any object of sight "high" or "low," in proportion as it is more or less distant from the visible earth. But to define the situation of visible things with relation to the distance they bear from any tangible thing, or vice versa, this were absurd and perfectly unintelligible. For all visible things are equally in the mind, and take up no part of the external space; and consequently are equidistant from any tangible thing which exists without the mind.

112. Or rather, to speak truly, the proper objects of sight are at no distance, neither near nor far from any tangible thing. For, if we inquire narrowly into the matter, we shall find that those things only are compared together in respect of distance which exist after the same manner, or appertain unto the same sense. For, by the distance between any two points, nothing more is meant than the number of intermediate points. If the given points are visible, the distance between them is marked out by the number of the interjacent visible points; if they are tangible, the distance between them is a line consisting of tangible points; but, if they are one tangible and the other visible, the distance between them neither consists of points perceivable by sight nor by touch, i.e., it is utterly inconceivable. This, perhaps, will not find an easy admission into all men's understanding. However, I should gladly be informed

whether it be not true, by anyone who will be at the pains to reflect a little, and apply it home to his thoughts.

113. The not observing what has been delivered in the two last sections seems to have occasioned no small part of the difficulty that occurs in the business of erect appearances. The head, which is painted nearest the earth, seems to be farthest from it; and on the other hand, the feet, which are painted farthest from the earth, are thought nearest to it. Herein lies the difficulty, which vanishes if we express the thing more clearly and free from ambiguity, thus: How comes it that, to the eye, the visible head, which is nearest the tangible earth, seems farthest from the earth; and the visible feet, which are farthest from the tangible earth, seem nearest the earth? The question being thus proposed, who sees not the difficulty is founded on a supposition that the eye or visive faculty, or rather the soul by means thereof, should judge of the situation of visible objects with reference to their distance from the tangible earth? Whereas, it is evident the tangible earth is not perceived by sight. And it has been shown in the two last preceding sections that the location of visible objects is determined only by the distance they bear from one another, and that it is nonsense to talk of distance, far or near, between a visible and tangible thing.

114. If we confine our thoughts to the proper objects of sight, the whole is plain and easy. The head is painted farthest from, and the feet nearest to, the visible earth; and so they appear to be. What is there strange or unaccountable in this? Let us suppose the pictures in the fund of the eye to be the immediate objects of the sight. The consequence is that things should appear in the same posture they are painted in; and is it not so? The head which is seen seems farthest from the earth which is seen; and the feet which are seen seem nearest to the earth which is seen. And just so they are painted.

115. But, say you, the picture of the man is inverted, and yet the appearance is erect. I ask, what mean you by the picture of the man or, which is the same thing, the visible man's being inverted? You tell me it is inverted because the heels are uppermost and the head undermost? Explain me this. You

say that by the heads being undermost, you mean that it is nearest to the earth; and, by the heels being uppermost, that they are farthest from the earth. I ask again, what earth [do] you mean? You cannot mean the earth that is painted on the eye or the visible earth—for the picture of the head is farthest from the picture of the earth, and the picture of the feet nearest to the picture of the earth; and accordingly the visible head is farthest from the visible earth, and the visible feet nearest to it. It remains, therefore, that you mean the tangible earth; and so determine the situation of visible things with respect to tangible things—contrary to what has been demonstrated in secs. 111 and 112. The two distinct provinces of sight and touch should be considered apart, and as if their objects had no intercourse, no manner of relation to one another, in point of distance or position.

116. Further, what greatly contributes to make us mistake in this matter is that when we think of the pictures in the fund of the eye, we imagine ourselves looking on the fund of another's eye, or another looking on the fund of our own eye, and beholding the pictures painted thereon. Suppose two eyes, *A* and *B*. *A* from some distance looking on the pictures in *B* sees them inverted, and for that reason concludes they are inverted in *B*. But this is wrong. There are projected in little on the bottom of *A* the images of the pictures of, suppose, man, earth, etc., which are painted on *B*. And besides these, the eye *B* itself, and the objects which environ it, together with another earth, are projected in a larger size on *A*. Now, by the eye *A* these larger images are deemed the true objects and the lesser only pictures in miniature. And it is with respect to those greater images that it determines the situation of the smaller images; so that, comparing the little man with the great earth, *A* judges him inverted, or that the feet are farthest from and the head nearest to the great earth. Whereas, if *A* compare the little man with the little earth, then he will appear erect, i.e., his head shall seem farthest from and his feet nearest to the little earth. But we must consider that *B* does not see two earths as *A* does. It sees only what is represented by the little pictures in *A*, and consequently shall judge the

man erect. For, in truth, the man in *B* is not inverted, for there the feet are next the earth; but it is the representation of it in *A* which is inverted, for there the head of the representation of the picture of the man in *B* is next the earth, and the feet farthest from the earth—meaning the earth which is without the representation of the pictures in *B*. For, if you take the little images of the pictures in *B*, and consider them by themselves, and with respect only to one another, they are all erect and in their natural posture.

117. Further, there lies a mistake in our imagining that the pictures of external objects are painted on the bottom of the eye. It has been shown there is no resemblance between the ideas of sight and things tangible. It has likewise been demonstrated that the proper objects of sight do not exist without the mind. Whence it clearly follows that the pictures painted on the bottom of the eye are not the pictures of external objects. Let anyone consult his own thoughts, and then say what affinity, what likeness, there is between that certain variety and disposition of colors, which constitute the visible man, or picture of a man, and that other combination of far different ideas, sensible by touch, which compose the tangible man. But if this be the case, how come they to be accounted pictures or images, since that supposes them to copy or represent some originals or other?

118. To which I answer: In the forementioned instance, the eye *A* takes the little images, included within the representation of the other eye *B*, to be pictures or copies whereof the archetypes are not things existing without, but the larger pictures projected on its own fund; and which by *A* are not thought pictures, but the originals or true things themselves. Though if we suppose a third eye *C*, from a due distance, to behold the fund of *A*, then indeed the things projected thereon shall, to *C*, seem pictures or images, in the same sense that those projected on *B* do to *A*.

119. Rightly to conceive this point [86] we must carefully distinguish between the ideas of sight and touch, between the

86 [This point—I, II: the business in hand.]

visible and tangible eye; for certainly on the tangible eye nothing either is or seems to be painted. Again, the visible eye, as well as all other visible objects, has been shown to exist only in the mind; which, perceiving its own ideas, and comparing them together, calls some "pictures" in respect to others. What has been said, being rightly comprehended and laid together, does, I think, afford a full and genuine explication of the erect appearance of objects—which phenomenon, I must confess, I do not see how it can be explained by any theories of vision hitherto made public.

120. In treating of these things, the use of language is apt to occasion some obscurity and confusion, and create in us wrong ideas. For, language being accommodated to the common notions and prejudices of men, it is scarce possible to deliver the naked and precise truth without great circumlocution, impropriety, and (to an unwary reader) seeming contradictions. I do, therefore, once for all, desire whoever shall think it worth his while to understand what I have written concerning vision, that he would not stick in this or that phrase or manner of expression, but candidly collect my meaning from the whole sum and tenor of my discourse, and laying aside the words as much as possible, consider the bare notions themselves, and then judge whether they are agreeable to truth and his own experience or no.

121. We have shown the way wherein the mind, by mediation of visible ideas, perceives or apprehends the distance, magnitude, and situation of tangible objects. We come now to inquire more particularly concerning the difference between the ideas of sight and touch which are called by the same names, and see whether there be any idea common to both senses.[87] From what we have at large set forth and demonstrated in the foregoing parts of this treatise, it is plain there is no one selfsame numerical extension, perceived both by sight and touch; but that the particular figures and exten-

[87] [Secs. 121-46. Cf. *Alciphron*, Dial. IV, secs. 10-12; *Visual Language*, secs. 41-46.]

sions perceived by sight, however they may be called by the same names and reputed the same things with those perceived by touch, are nevertheless different, and have an existence distinct and separate from them. So that the question is not now concerning the same numerical ideas, but whether there be any one and the same sort or species of ideas equally perceivable to both senses? Or, in other words, whether extension, figure, and motion perceived by sight, are not specifically distinct from extension, figure, and motion perceived by touch?

122. But before I come more particularly to discuss this matter, I find it proper to consider [88] extension in abstract.[89] For of this there is much talk; and I am apt to think that when men speak of extension as being an idea common to two senses, it is with a secret supposition that we can single out extension from all other tangible and visible qualities, and form thereof an abstract idea, which idea they will have common both to sight and touch. We are therefore to understand by extension in abstract, an idea of extension—for instance, a line or surface entirely stripped of all other sensible qualities and circumstances that might determine it to any particular existence; it is neither black, nor white, nor red, nor has it any color at all, or any tangible quality whatsoever, and consequently it is of no finite determinate magnitude; for that which bounds or distinguishes one extension from another is some quality or circumstance wherein they disagree.

123. Now, I do not find that I can perceive, imagine, or anywise frame in my mind such an abstract idea as is here spoken of. A line or surface which is neither black, nor white, nor blue, nor yellow, etc., nor long, nor short, nor rough, nor smooth, nor square, nor round, etc., is perfectly incomprehensible. This I am sure of as to myself; how far the faculties of other men may reach they best can tell.

124. It is [90] commonly said that the object of geometry is ab-

88 [Consider—I, II: take into my thoughts.]

89 [On abstract ideas cf. also *Alciphron*, Dial. VII, secs. 5-8; *Visual Language*, sec. 47; *Principles*, Introduction, secs. 6-20.]

90 [It is—I, II: I know it is.]

stract extension. But [91] geometry contemplates figures: now, figure is the termination of magnitude; but we have shown that extension in abstract has no finite determinate magnitude; whence it clearly follows that it can have no figure, and consequently is not the object of geometry. It is indeed a tenet, as well of the modern as of the ancient philosophers, that all general truths are concerning universal abstract ideas; without which, we are told, there could be no science, no demonstration of any general proposition in geometry. But it were no hard matter, did I think it necessary to my present purpose, to show that propositions and demonstrations in geometry might be universal, though they who make them never think of abstract general ideas of triangles or circles.

125. After reiterated endeavors to [92] apprehend the general idea of a triangle, I have found it altogether incomprehensible. And surely, if anyone were able to introduce that idea into my mind, it must be the author [93] of the *Essay Concerning Human Understanding:* he, who has so far distinguished himself from the generality of writers by the clearness and significancy of what he says. Let us therefore see how this celebrated author [94] describes the general or abstract [95] idea of a triangle. "It must be," says he, "neither oblique nor rectangular, neither equilateral, equicrural, nor scalenum; but all and none of these at once. In effect it is somewhat imperfect that cannot exist; an idea, wherein some parts of several different and inconsistent ideas are put together." (*Essay on Human Understanding*, Bk. IV, chap. 7, sec. 9.) This is the idea which

91 [But—I, II: To this I cannot agree; for.]

92 [Endeavors to—I, II: efforts and pangs of thought in order to.]

93 [Author—I, II: deservedly admired author.—John Locke (1632-1704). He published his *Essay* first in 1690; his revolutionary book was available to Berkeley when he entered Trinity College, Dublin, in 1700, at the early age of fifteen. A. A. Luce says that Locke's famous work "went on the course almost at once, . . . and was working like leaven" (*Life of George Berkeley* [Edinburgh, 1949], p. 31). What follows is Berkeley's first argument against Locke's doctrine of abstract ideas.]

94 [This celebrated author—I, II: that great man.]

95 [Or abstract—I, II: or, which is the same thing, one.]

he thinks needful for the enlargement of knowledge, which is the subject of mathematical demonstration, and without which we could never come to know any general proposition concerning triangles.[96] That author acknowledges it does "require some pains and skill to form this general idea of a triangle." (*Ibid.*) But, had he called to mind what he says in another place, to wit, "that ideas of mixed modes wherein any inconsistent ideas are put together cannot so much as exist in the mind, i.e., be conceived" (*vide* Bk. III, chap. 10, sec. 33, *ibid.*)—I say, had this occurred to his thoughts, it is not improbable he would have owned it above all the pains and skill he was master of, to form the above-mentioned idea of a triangle, which is made up of manifest staring contradictions. That a man who laid [97] so great a stress on clear and determinate ideas should nevertheless talk at this rate seems very surprising. But the wonder will lessen if it be considered [98] that the source whence this opinion [99] flows is the prolific womb which has brought forth innumerable errors and difficulties, in all parts of philosophy, and in all the sciences. But this matter, taken in its full extent, were a subject too comprehensive [100] to be insisted on in this place.[101] And so much for extension in abstract.

96 [Concerning triangles.—I, II: concerning triangles. Sure I am, if this be the case, 'tis impossible for me to attain to know even the first elements of geometry, since I have not the faculty to frame in my mind such an idea as is here described.]

97 [Who laid—I, II: of such a clear understanding, who thought so much, and so well, and laid—III: who thought so much and laid.]

98 [But the wonder will lessen if it be considered—I, II: But my wonder is lessened when I consider.]

99 [This opinion—I, II: this opinion of abstract figures and extension.]

100 [Too comprehensive—I, II: too vast and comprehensive.]

101 [This place.—I, II: this place. I shall only observe that your metaphysicians and men of speculation seem to have faculties distinct from those of ordinary men, when they talk of general or abstracted triangles and circles, etc. and so peremptorily declare them to be the subject of all the eternal, immutable, universal truths in geometry.]

126. Some, perhaps, may think pure space, vacuum, or trine dimension to be equally the object of sight and touch. But, though we have a very great propension to think the ideas of outness and space to be the immediate object of sight, yet, if I mistake not, in the foregoing parts of this essay that has been clearly demonstrated to be a mere delusion, arising from the quick and sudden suggestion of fancy, which so closely connects the idea of distance with that of sight that we are apt to think it is itself a proper and immediate object of that sense, till reason corrects the mistake.

127. It having been shown that there are no abstract ideas of figure, and that it is impossible for us, by any precision of thought, to frame an idea of extension separate from all other visible and tangible qualities which shall be common both to sight and touch, the question now remaining is whether the particular extensions, figures, and motions perceived by sight be of the same kind with the particular extensions, figures, and motions perceived by touch? In answer to which I shall venture to lay down the following proposition: *The extension, figures, and motions perceived by sight are specifically distinct from the ideas of touch, called by the same names; nor is there any such thing as one idea, or kind of idea, common to both senses.*[102] This proposition may, without much difficulty, be collected from what has been said in several places of this essay. But, because it seems so remote from, and contrary to, the received notions and settled opinion of mankind, I shall attempt to demonstrate it more particularly and at large by the following arguments.

128. When upon [103] perception of an idea I range it under this or that sort, it is because it is perceived after the same

[102] [This conclusion of the previous analysis later becomes, in the theory, "the main part and pillar" (*Visual Language*, sec. 41). Cf. Descartes' *Regulae* (1st edn.; Amsterdam, 1701), Bk. XII: "shape which is both seen and felt"; and Locke's *Essay*, Bk. II, chap. xiii, sec. 2: "We get the idea of space both by our sight and touch."]

[103] [When upon—I, II: *First*, when upon.]

manner, or because it has a likeness or conformity with, or affects me in the same way as the ideas of the sort I rank it under. In short, it must not be entirely new, but have something in it old and already perceived by me. It must, I say, have so much, at least, in common with the ideas I have before known and named as to make me give it the same name with them. But, it has been, if I mistake not, clearly made out that a man born blind would not, at first reception of his sight, think the things he saw were of the same nature with the objects of touch, or had anything in common with them; but that they were a new set of ideas, perceived in a new manner, and entirely different from all he had ever perceived before. So that he would not call them by the same name, nor repute them to be of the same sort, with anything he had hitherto known.[104]

129. *Secondly*, light and colors are allowed by all to constitute a sort of species entirely different from the ideas of touch; nor will any man, I presume, say they can make themselves perceived by that sense. But there is no other immediate object of sight besides light and colors. It is therefore a direct consequence that there is no idea common to both senses.

130. It is a prevailing opinion, even amongst those who have thought and written most accurately concerning our ideas, and the ways whereby they enter into the understanding, that something more is perceived by sight than barely light and colors with their variations. Mr. Locke [105] terms sight "the most comprehensive of all our senses, conveying to our minds the ideas of light and colors, which are peculiar only to that sense; and also the far different ideas of space, figure, and motion." (*Essay on Human Understanding*, Bk. II, chap. 9,

[104] [Hitherto known.—I, II: hitherto known. And surely the judgment of such an unprejudiced person is more to be relied on in this case than the sentiments of the generality of men who, in this as in almost everything else, suffer themselves to be guided by custom, and the erroneous suggestions of prejudice, rather than reason and sedate reflection.]

[105] [Mr. Locke—I, II: The excellent Mr. Locke.]

sec. 9.) Space or distance, we have shown, is not otherwise the object of sight than of hearing (*vide* sec. 46). And as for figure and extension, I leave it to anyone that shall calmly attend to his own clear and distinct ideas to decide whether he has any idea intromitted immediately and properly by sight save only light and colors; or whether it be possible for him to frame in his mind a distinct abstract idea of visible extension, or figure, exclusive of all color; and, on the other hand, whether he can conceive color without visible extension? For my own part, I must confess, I am not able to attain so great a nicety of abstraction; in a strict sense,[106] I see nothing but light and colors, with their several shades and variations. He who beside these also perceives by sight ideas far different and distinct from them, has that faculty in a degree more perfect and comprehensive than I can pretend to. It must be owned that,[107] by the mediation of light and colors, other far different ideas are suggested to my mind: but so they are by hearing [108] which, beside sounds which are peculiar to that sense, does, by their mediation, suggest not only space, figure, and motion, but also all other ideas whatsoever that can be signified by words.

131. *Thirdly,* it is, I think, an axiom universally received that quantities of the same kind may be added together and make one entire sum. Mathematicians add lines together; but they do not add a line to a solid, or conceive it as making one sum with a surface. These three kinds of quantity being thought incapable of any such mutual addition, and consequently of being compared together in the several ways of proportion, are by them esteemed [109] entirely disparate and heterogeneous. Now let anyone try in his thoughts to add a visible line or surface to a tangible line or surface so as to

106 [In a strict sense—I, II: I know very well that in a strict sense.]

107 [It must be owned that—I, II: I own indeed.]

108 [But so they are by hearing—I, II: but then, upon this score, I see no reason why the sight should be thought more comprehensive than the hearing.]

109 [By them esteemed—I, II: by them for that reason esteemed.]

conceive them making one continued sum or whole. He that can do this may think them homogeneous; but he that cannot must, by the foregoing axiom, think them heterogeneous.[110] A blue and a red line I can conceive added together into one sum and making one continued line; but, to make, in my thoughts, one continued line of a visible and tangible line added together is, I find, a task far more difficult, and even insurmountable; and I leave it to the reflection and experience of every particular person to determine for himself.

132. A further confirmation of our tenet may be drawn from the solution of Mr. Molyneux's [111] problem, published by Mr. Locke in his *Essay*: which I shall set down as it there lies, together with Mr. Locke's opinion of it: "*Suppose a man born blind, and now adult, and taught by his touch to distinguish between a cube and a sphere of the same metal, and nighly*

[110] [Heterogeneous—I, II: heterogeneous. I acknowledge myself to be of the latter sort.]

[111] [William Molyneux (1655-98) published his *New Dioptrics* in 1692. He corresponded with Locke in the 'nineties and introduced Locke's *Essay* to Trinity College, Dublin, before Locke was known at Oxford or Cambridge. He sent his "jocose problem" to Locke on March 2, 1693. Locke published it in the second edition of the *Essay*, Bk. II, chap. ix, sec. 8. Later Molyneux described to Locke how his friends were led to give the wrong solution to his problem, the main false step being "the same name" of the two objects. See Locke's *Some Familiar Letters . . .* (London, 1706). Cf. also Gottfried Wilhelm von Leibniz' *New Essays,* translated by A. G. Langley (London, 1894), Bk. II, chap. 9, sec. 8, from *Nouveaux essais sur l'entendement humain,* a long dialogue composed in 1703 in reply to Locke's *Essay* but not published until 1765 by Raspe in *Oeuvres philosophiques latines et françoises* (Amsterdam and Leipzig). Leibniz maintained that since shape is common to sight and touch, the once-blind man could recognize the cube by the principles of reason. He argued that we all possess "a natural geometry." See Marius von Senden's *Space and Sight* (Glencoe, 1960), translated by Peter Heath from the German edition (1932), pp. 295, 299, etc. Von Senden says that "the patient's visual field contains nothing beyond a set of perfectly genuine visual objects, which are still devoid of any significance," that "these visual impressions awaken no familiar ideas in him, and that he cannot recognize the objects in question." Cf. J. J. Gibson's *The Perception of the Visual World* (Boston, 1950), p. 217; and *Visual Language,* sec. 71.]

of the same bigness, so as to tell when he felt one and the other, which is the cube, and which the sphere. Suppose then the cube and sphere placed on a table, and the blind man made to see: quaere, *whether by his sight, before he touched them, he could now distinguish and tell which is the globe, which the cube?* To which the acute and judicious proposer answers: *Not. For, though he has obtained the experience of how a globe, how a cube affects his touch; yet he has not yet attained the experience that what affects his touch so or so must affect his sight so or so; or that a protuberant angle in the cube, that pressed his hand unequally, shall appear to his eye as it does in the cube.* I agree with this thinking gentleman, whom I am proud to call my friend, in his answer to this his problem; and am of opinion that the blind man, at first sight, would not be able with certainty to say which was the globe, which the cube, while he only saw them" (*Essay on Human Understanding,* Bk. II, chap. 9, sec. 8).

133. Now, if a square surface perceived by touch be the same sort with a square surface perceived by sight, it is certain the blind man here mentioned might know a square surface as soon as he saw it. It is no more but introducing into his mind, by a new inlet, an idea he has been already well acquainted with. Since therefore he is supposed to have known by his touch that a cube is a body terminated by square surfaces; and that a sphere is not terminated by square surfaces—upon the supposition that a visible and tangible square differ only *in numero,* it follows that he might know, by the unerring mark of the square surfaces, which was the cube, and which not, while he only saw them. We must therefore allow either that visible extension and figures are specifically distinct from tangible extension and figures, or else that the solution of this problem given by those two thoughtful [112] and ingenious men is wrong.

134. Much more might be laid together in proof of the proposition I have advanced. But, what has been said is, if I mis-

[112] [Two thoughtful—I, II: two very thoughtful.]

take not, sufficient to convince anyone that shall yield a reasonable attention. And, as for those that will not be at the pains of a little thought, no multiplication of words will ever suffice to make them understand the truth or rightly conceive my meaning.

135. I cannot let go the above-mentioned problem without some reflection on it. It has been made evident that a man blind from his birth would not, at first sight, denominate anything he saw by the names he had been used to appropriate to ideas of touch (*vide* sec. 106). "Cube," "sphere," "table," are words he has known applied to things perceivable by touch, but to things perfectly intangible he never knew them applied. Those words, in their wonted application, always marked out to his mind bodies or solid things which were perceived by the resistance they gave. But there is no solidity, no resistance or protrusion, perceived by sight. In short, the ideas of sight are all new perceptions to which there be no names annexed in his mind; he cannot therefore understand what is said to him concerning them. And to ask of the two bodies he saw placed on the table which was the sphere, which the cube, were to him a question downright bantering and unintelligible, nothing he sees being able to suggest to his thoughts the idea of body, distance, or, in general, of anything he had already known.

136. It is a mistake to think the same thing affects both sight and touch. If the same angle or square which is the object of touch be also the object of vision, what should hinder the blind man, at first sight, from knowing it? For, though the manner wherein it affects the sight be different from that wherein it affected his touch, yet, there being beside this manner or circumstance which is new and unknown the angle or figure which is old and known, he cannot choose but discern it.

137. Visible figure and extension having been demonstrated to be of a nature entirely different and heterogeneous from tangible figure and extension, it remains that we inquire con-

cerning motion. Now, that visible motion is not of the same sort with tangible motion seems to need no further proof; it being an evident corollary from what we have shown concerning the difference there is betwixt visible and tangible extension. But for a more full and express proof hereof, we need only observe that one who had not yet experienced vision would not at first sight know motion. Whence it clearly follows that motion perceivable by sight is of a sort distinct from motion perceivable by touch. The antecedent I prove thus: By touch he could not perceive any motion but what was up or down, to the right or left, nearer or farther from him; besides these, and their several varieties or complications, it is impossible he should have any idea of motion. He would not therefore think anything to be motion, or give the name "motion" to any idea which he could not range under some or other of those particular kinds thereof. But from sec. 95 it is plain that, by the mere act of vision, he could not know motion upward or downward, to the right or left, or in any other possible direction. From which I conclude, he would not know motion at all at first sight. As for the idea of motion in abstract, I shall not waste paper about it, but leave it to my reader to make the best he can of it. To me it is perfectly unintelligible.

138. The consideration of motion may furnish a new field for inquiry. But, since the manner wherein the mind apprehends by sight the motion of tangible objects, with the various degrees thereof, may be easily collected from what has been said concerning the manner wherein that sense does suggest their various distances, magnitudes, and situations, I shall not enlarge any further on this subject, but proceed to consider [113] what may be alleged with greatest appearance of reason, against the proposition we have shown [114] to be true: For, where there is so much prejudice to be encountered, a

113 [Consider—I, II, III: inquire.]
114 [Shown—I, II: demonstrated.]

bare and naked demonstration of the truth will scarce suffice. We must also satisfy the scruples that men may raise [115] in favor of their preconceived notions, show whence the mistake arises, how it came to spread, and carefully disclose and root out those false persuasions that an early prejudice might have implanted in the mind.

139. *First,* therefore, it will be demanded how visible extension and figures come to be called by the same name with tangible extension and figures, if they are not of the same kind with them? It must be something more than humor or accident that could occasion a custom so constant and universal as this, which has obtained in all ages and nations of the world, and amongst all ranks of men, the learned as well as the illiterate.

140. To which I answer, we can no more argue a visible and tangible square to be of the same species from their being called by the same name, than we can that a tangible square and the monosyllable consisting of six letters whereby it is marked are of the same species, because they are both called by the same name. It is customary to call written words and the things they signify by the same name; for, words not being regarded in their own nature, or otherwise than as they are marks of things, it had been superfluous and beside the design of language to have given them names distinct from those of the things marked by them. The same reason holds here also. Visible figures are the marks of tangible figures; and, from sec. 59, it is plain that in themselves they are little regarded, or upon any other score than for their connection with tangible figures, which by nature they are ordained to signify. And, because this language of nature does not vary in different ages or nations, hence it is that in all times and places visible figures are called by the same names as the respective tangible figures suggested by them; and not because they are alike, or of the same sort with them.

141. But, say you, surely a tangible square is liker to a

115 [Raise—I, II: start.]

visible square than to a visible circle: It has four angles, and as many sides; so also has the visible square; but the visible circle has no such thing, being bounded by one uniform curve, without right lines or angles, which makes it unfit to represent the tangible square, but very fit to represent the tangible circle. Whence it clearly follows that visible figures are patterns of, or of the same species with, the respective tangible figures represented by them; that they are like unto them, and of their own nature fitted to represent them, as being of the same sort; and that they are in no respect arbitrary signs, as words.

142. I answer, it must be acknowledged the visible square is fitter than the visible circle to represent the tangible square, but then it is not because it is liker, or more of a species with it, but because the visible square contains in it several distinct parts whereby to mark the several distinct corresponding parts of a tangible square, whereas the visible circle does not. The square perceived by touch has four distinct equal sides, so also has it four distinct equal angles. It is therefore necessary that the visible figure which shall be most proper to mark it contain four distinct equal parts, corresponding to the four sides of the tangible square; as likewise four other distinct and equal parts, whereby to denote the four equal angles of the tangible square. And accordingly we see the visible figures contain in them distinct visible parts, answering to the distinct tangible parts of the figures signified or suggested by them.

143. But it will not hence follow that any visible figure is like unto or of the same species with its corresponding tangible figure—unless it be also shown that not only the number but also the kind of the parts be the same in both. To illustrate this, I observe that visible figures represent tangible figures much after the same manner that written words do sounds. Now, in this respect, words are not arbitrary; it not being indifferent what written word stands for any sound. But it is requisite that each word contain in it so many distinct characters as there are variations in the sound it stands for. Thus, the single letter "a" is proper to mark one simple

uniform sound; and the word "adultery" is accommodated
to represent the sound annexed to it—in the formation
whereof, there being eight different collisions or modifications
of the air by the organs of speech, each of which produces a
difference of sound, it was fit the word representing it should
consist of as many distinct characters, thereby to mark each
particular difference or part of the whole sound. And yet nobody, I presume, will say the single letter "a," or the word
"adultery," are alike unto or of the same species with the
respective sounds by them represented. It is indeed arbitrary
that, in general, letters of any language represent sounds at
all; but, when that is once agreed, it is not arbitrary what
combination of letters shall represent this or that particular
sound. I leave this with the reader to pursue, and apply it in
his own thoughts.

144. It must be confessed that we are not so apt to confound other signs with the things signified, or to think them
of the same species, as we are visible and tangible ideas. But,
a little consideration will show us how this may be, without
our supposing them of a like nature. These signs are constant
and universal; their connection with tangible ideas has been
learned at our first entrance into the world; and ever since,
almost every moment of our lives, it has been occurring to our
thoughts, and fastening and striking deeper on our minds.
When we observe that signs are variable, and of human institution; when we remember there was a time they were not
connected in our minds with those things they now so readily
suggest, but that their signification was learned by the slow
steps of experience: this preserves us from confounding them.
But, when we find the same signs suggest the same things all
over the world; when we know they are not of human institution, and cannot remember that we ever learned their signification, but think that at first sight they would have suggested
to us the same things they do now—all this persuades us they
are of the same species as the things respectively represented
by them, and that it is by a natural resemblance they suggest
them to our minds.

145. Add to this that whenever we make a nice survey of any object, successively directing the optic axis to each point thereof, there are certain lines and figures, described by the motion of the head or eye which, being in truth perceived by feeling, do nevertheless so mix themselves, as it were, with the ideas of sight that we can scarce think but they appertain to that sense. Again, the ideas of sight enter into the mind several at once, more distinct and unmingled than is usual in the other senses beside the touch. Sounds, for example, perceived at the same instant, are apt to coalesce, if I may so say, into one sound; but we can perceive, at the same time, great variety of visible objects, very separate and distinct from each other. Now, tangible extension being made up of several distinct coexistent parts, we may hence gather another reason that may dispose us to imagine a likeness or analogy between the immediate objects of sight and touch. But nothing, certainly, does more contribute to blend and confound them together than the strict and close connection they have with each other. We cannot open our eyes but the ideas of distance, bodies, and tangible figures are suggested by them. So swift, and sudden, and unperceived is the transition from visible to tangible ideas that we can scarce forbear thinking them equally the immediate object of vision.

146. The prejudice which is grounded on these, and whatever other causes may be assigned thereof, sticks so fast [116] that it is impossible, without obstinate striving and labor of the mind, to get entirely clear of it. But then the reluctancy we find in rejecting any opinion can be no argument of its truth, to whoever considers what has been already shown with regard to the prejudices we entertain concerning the distance, magnitude, and situation of objects; prejudices so familiar to our minds, so confirmed and inveterate, as they will hardly give way to the clearest demonstration.

147. Upon the whole, I think we may fairly conclude [117]

116 [So fast—I, II: so fast on our understandings.]

117 [The ultimate conclusion of Berkeley's analysis, later assumed as the principle in the theory of vision. See *Visual Language*, sec. 38.]

that the proper objects of vision constitute a universal language of the Author of nature,[118] whereby we are instructed how to regulate our actions in order to attain those things that are necessary to the preservation and well-being of our bodies, as also to avoid whatever may be hurtful and destructive of them. It is by their information that we are principally guided in all the transactions and concerns of life. And the manner wherein they signify and mark unto us the objects which are at a distance is the same with that of languages and signs of human appointment; which do not suggest the things signified by any likeness or identity of nature, but only by a habitual connection that experience has made us to observe between them.

148. Suppose one who had always continued blind be told by his guide that after he has advanced so many steps he shall come to the brink of a precipice, or be stopped by a wall; must not this to him seem very admirable and surprising? He cannot conceive how it is possible for mortals to frame such predictions as these, which to him seem as strange and unaccountable as prophecy does to others. Even they who are blessed with the visive faculty may (though familiarity make it less observed) find therein sufficient cause of admiration. The wonderful art and contrivance wherewith it is adjusted to those ends and purposes for which it was apparently designed; the vast extent, number, and variety of objects that are at once, with so much ease, and quickness, and pleasure, suggested by it—all these afford subject for much and pleasing speculation, and may, if anything, give us some glimmering analogous prenotion of things that are placed beyond the certain discovery and comprehension of our present state.

149. I do not design to trouble myself with drawing corollaries from the doctrine I have hitherto laid down. If it bears the test, others may, so far as they shall think convenient, employ their thoughts in extending it further, and applying it to whatever purposes it may be subservient to. Only, I cannot

---

[118] [A universal language of the Author of nature,—I, II: the universal language of nature.]

forbear making some inquiry concerning the object of geometry, which the subject we have been upon does naturally lead one to. We have shown there is no such idea as that of extension in abstract; and that there are two kinds of sensible extension and figures, which are entirely distinct and heterogeneous from each other. Now, it is natural to inquire which of these is the object of geometry.

150. Some things there are which, at first sight, incline one to think geometry conversant about visible extension. The constant use of the eyes, both in the practical and speculative parts of that science, does very much induce us thereto. It would without doubt seem odd to a mathematician to go about to convince him the diagrams he saw upon paper were not the figures, or even the likeness of the figures, which make the subject of the demonstration—the contrary being held an unquestionable truth not only by mathematicians but also by those who apply themselves more particularly to the study of logic; I mean, who consider the nature of science, certainty, and demonstration; it being by them assigned as one reason of the extraordinary clearness and evidence of geometry, that in this science the reasonings are free from those inconveniences which attend the use of arbitrary signs, the very ideas themselves being copied out and exposed to view upon paper. But, by the bye, how well this agrees with what they likewise assert of abstract ideas being the object of geometrical demonstration I leave to be considered.

151. To come to a resolution in this point, we need only observe what has been said in secs. 59, 60, 61, where it is shown that visible extensions in themselves are little regarded and have no settled determinate greatness, and that men measure altogether by the application of tangible extension to tangible extension. All which makes it evident that visible extension and figures are not the object of geometry.

152. It is therefore plain that visible figures are of the same use in geometry that words are. And the one may as well be accounted the object of that science as the other; neither of them being otherwise concerned therein than as they represent

or suggest to the mind the particular tangible figures connected with them. There is, indeed, this difference betwixt the
signification of tangible figures by visible figures, and of ideas
by words—that whereas the latter is variable and uncertain,
depending altogether on the arbitrary appointment of men,
the former is fixed and immutably the same in all times and
places. A visible square, for instance, suggests to the mind the
same tangible figure in Europe that it does in America. Hence
it is that the voice of the Author of nature,[119] which speaks
to our eyes, is not liable to that misinterpretation and ambiguity that languages of human contrivance are unavoidably
subject to.[120]

153. Though what has been said may suffice to show what
ought to be determined with relation to the object of geometry, I shall, nevertheless, for the fuller illustration thereof,
consider the case of an intelligence or unbodied spirit, which
is supposed to see perfectly well, i.e., to have a clear perception
of the proper and immediate objects of sight, but to have no
sense of touch. Whether there be any such being in nature or
no is beside my purpose to inquire; it suffices that the supposition contains no contradiction in it. Let us now examine what
proficiency such a one may be able to make in geometry. Which
speculation will lead us more clearly to see whether the ideas
of sight can possibly be the object of that science.

154. *First,* then, it is certain the aforesaid intelligence could
have no idea of a solid or quantity of three dimensions, which
follows from its not having any idea of distance. We, indeed,
are prone to think that we have by sight the ideas of space
and solids; which arises from our imagining that we do, strictly
speaking, see distance, and some parts of an object at a greater
distance than others; which has been demonstrated to be the
effect of the experience we have had what ideas of touch are
connected with such and such ideas attending vision. But the
intelligence here spoken of is supposed to have no experience

119 [The Author of nature—I, II: nature.]

120 [Subject to.—I, II: subjected to. From which may, in some measure,
be derived that peculiar evidence and clearness of geometrical demonstrations.]

of touch. He would not, therefore, judge as we do, nor have any idea of distance, outness, or profundity, nor consequently of space or body, either immediately or by suggestion. Whence it is plain he can have no notion of those parts of geometry which relate to the mensuration of solids, and their convex or concave surfaces, and contemplate the properties of lines generated by the section of a solid. The conceiving of any part whereof is beyond the reach of his faculties.

155. *Further*, he cannot comprehend the manner wherein geometers describe a right line or circle; the rule and compass, with their use, being things of which it is impossible he should have any notion. Nor is it an easier matter for him to conceive the placing of one plane or angle on another in order to prove their equality, since that supposes some idea of distance, or external space. All which makes it evident our pure intelligence could never attain to know so much as the first elements of plane geometry. And perhaps, upon a nice inquiry, it will be found he cannot even have an idea of plane figures any more than he can of solids, since some idea of distance is necessary to form the idea of a geometrical plane, as will appear to whoever shall reflect a little on it.

156. All that is properly perceived by the visive faculty amounts to no more than colors with their variations, and different proportions of light and shade—but the perpetual mutability and fleetingness of those immediate objects of sight render them incapable of being managed after the manner of geometrical figures; nor is it in any degree useful that they should. It is true there are divers of them perceived at once, and more of some, and less of others; but accurately to compute their magnitude, and assign precise determinate proportions between things so variable and inconstant, if we suppose it possible to be done, must yet be a very trifling and insignificant labor.

157. I must confess men are tempted to think [121] that flat or plane figures are immediate objects of sight, though they

121 [Men are tempted to think—I, II: it seems to be the opinion of some very ingenious men—III: it seems to be the opinion of some ingenious men.]

acknowledge solids are not. And this opinion is grounded on what is observed in painting, wherein it seems the ideas immediately printed on the mind are only of planes variously colored, which, by a sudden act of the judgment, are changed into solids; but, with a little attention, we shall find the planes here mentioned as the immediate objects of sight are not visible but tangible planes. For, when we say that pictures are planes we mean thereby that they appear to the touch smooth and uniform. But then this smoothness and uniformity or, in other words, this planeness of the picture is not perceived immediately by vision; for it appears to the eye various and multiform.

158. From all which we may conclude that planes are no more the immediate object of sight than solids.[122] What we strictly see are not solids, nor yet planes variously colored—they are only diversity of colors. And some of these suggest to the mind solids, and others plane figures, just as they have been experienced to be connected with the one or the other; so that we see planes in the same way that we see solids—both being equally suggested by the immediate objects of sight, which accordingly are themselves denominated "planes" and "solids." But, though they are called by the same names with the things marked by them, they are, nevertheless, of a nature entirely different, as has been demonstrated.

159. What has been said is, if I mistake not, sufficient to decide the question we proposed to examine, concerning the ability of a pure spirit, such as we have described, to know geometry. It is, indeed, no easy matter for us to enter precisely into the thoughts of such an intelligence; because we cannot, without great pains, cleverly separate and disentangle in our thoughts the proper objects of sight from those of touch which are connected with them. This, indeed, in a complete degree

---

122 [Cf. Bertrand Russell: "Berkeley's theory of vision, according to which everything looks flat, is disproved by the stereoscope" (*Human Knowledge* [London, 1948], p. 51). But cf. also Mill (*Dissertations*, II, 165), and Armstrong: "A merely two-dimensional manifold is not flat" (*Berkeley's Theory of Vision*, p. 6).]

seems scarce possible to be performed, which will not seem strange to us, if we consider how hard it is for anyone to hear the words of his native language [123] pronounced in his ears without understanding them. Though he endeavor to disunite the meaning from the sound, it will nevertheless intrude into his thoughts, and he shall find it extremely difficult, if not impossible, to put himself exactly in the posture of a foreigner that never learned the language, so as to be affected barely with the sounds themselves and not perceive the signification annexed to them.[124] By this time, I suppose, it is clear that neither abstract nor visible extension makes the object of geometry; the not discerning of which may, perhaps, have created some difficulty and useless labor in mathematics.[125]

[123] [Native language—I, II: native language, which is familiar to him.]

[124] [By this—I, II: begin new section, 160, at this point.]

[125] [In mathematics.—I, II: in mathematics. Sure I am that somewhat relating thereto has occurred to my thoughts; which though after the most anxious and repeated examination I am forced to think it true does nevertheless seem so far out of the common road of geometry, that I know not whether it may not be thought presumption if I should make it public in an age wherein that science has received such mighty improvements by new methods; great part whereof, as well as of the ancient discoveries, may perhaps lose their reputation and much of that ardor with which men study the abstruse and fine geometry be abated, if what to me, and those few to whom I have imparted it, seems evidently true, should really prove to be so.]

AN APPENDIX [1]

The censures which, I am informed, have been made on the foregoing essay inclined me to think I had not been clear and express enough in some points, and to prevent being misunderstood for the future I was willing to make any necessary alterations or additions in what I had written. But that was impracticable, the present edition having been almost finished before I received this information. Wherefore I think it proper to consider in this place the principal objections that come to my notice.

In the first place it's objected that in the beginning of the essay I argue either against all use of lines and angles in optics, and then what I say is false; or against those writers only who will have it that we can perceive by sense the optic axes, angles, etc., and then it's insignificant, this being an absurdity which no one ever held. To which I answer that I argue only against those who are of opinion that we perceive the distance of objects by lines and angles or, as they term it, by a kind of innate geometry. And to show that this is not fighting with my own shadow, I shall here set down a passage from the celebrated Descartes.[2]

Distantiam praeterea discimus, per mutuam quandam conspirationem oculorum. Ut enim caecus noster duo bacilla tenens AE et CE, de quorum longitudine incertus, solumque intervallum manuum A et C, cum magnitudine angulorum ACE, et CAE exploratum habens, inde, ut ex geometria quadam omnibus innata, scire potest ubi sit punctum E. Sic quum nostri oculi RST et *rst* ambo, vertuntur ad X,

1 [In the second edition only. Berkeley wrote to Percival on March 1, 1710: "In an appendix I have endeavored to answer the objections of the Archbishop of Dublin." The archbishop was William King (1650-1729), the author of *The Origin of Evil*, translated by E. Law (London, 1731), from *De Origine Mali* (Dublin, 1702), and *Divine Predestination and Foreknowledge,* a sermon (on Romans 8:29, 30) preached at Christ Church, Dublin, May 15, 1709 (published in Dublin, 1709).]

2 [From Descartes' *Dioptrics*, Discourse VI, sec. 13.]

magnitudo lineae S*s*, et angulorum XS*s* et X*s*S, certos nos reddunt ubi sit punctum X. Et idem opera alterutrius possumus indagare, loco illum movendo, ut si versus X illum semper dirigentes, primo sistamus in puncto S, et statim post in puncto *s*, hoc sufficiet ut magnitudo lineae S*s*, et duorum angulorum XS*s* et X*s*S nostrae imaginationi simul occurrant, et distantiam puncti X nos edoceant; idque per actionem mentis, quae licet simplex judicium esse videatur, ratiocinationem tamen quandam involutam habet, similem illi, qua geometrae per duas stationes diversas, loca inaccessa dimetiuntur.[3]

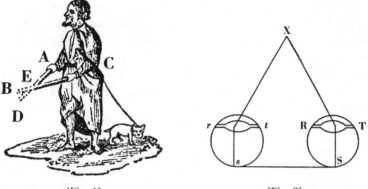

[Fig. 1]   [Fig. 2]

[3] ["Moreover, we perceive distance by means of the reciprocal union of the eyes. Our blind man [Fig. 1], holding the two sticks AE and CE whose lengths he is ignorant of and having established only the distance AC between his hands and the size of the angles ACE and CAE, is able to perceive, as it were by natural geometry, where the point E is. In similar fashion, if our two eyes [Fig. 2] RST and *rst* are turned toward the point X, then, from the length of the line S*s* and the size of the angles XS*s* and X*s*S, we are able to perceive where the point X is. We can accomplish the same thing by using either one or the other eye if we change its place. If we keep the eye directed toward X and place it first at the point S and then at the point *s*, this is sufficient to enable us to imagine the coexistence of the length of the line S*s* and the size of the angles XS*s* and X*s*S, and thus to perceive the distance of the point X. The act of the mind that achieves this seems to be a simple judgment characterized, however, by intricate reasoning similar to that done by geometers who from two separate positions estimate inaccessible places."]

I might amass together citations from several authors to the same purpose, but this being so clear in the point, and from an author of so great note, I shall not trouble the reader with any more. What I have said on this head was not for the sake of finding fault with other men, but because I judged it necessary to demonstrate in the first place that we neither see distance immediately, nor yet perceive it by the mediation of anything that has (as lines and angles) a necessary connection with it. For on the demonstration of this point the whole theory depends.

Secondly, it is objected that the explication I give of the appearance of the horizontal moon (which may also be applied to the sun) is the same that Gassendus had given before. I answer, there is indeed mention made of the grossness of the atmosphere in both, but then the methods wherein it is applied to solve the phenomenon are widely different, as will be evident to whoever shall compare what I have said on this subject with the following words of Gassendus:

> Heinc dici posse videtur: solem humilem oculo spectatum ideo apparere majorem, quam dum altius egreditur, quia dum vicinus est horizonti prolixa est series vaporum, atque adeo corpusculorum quae solis radios ita retundunt, ut oculus minus conniveat, et pupilla quasi umbrefacta longe magis amplificetur, quam dum sole multum elato rari vapores intercipiuntur, solque ipse ita splendescit, ut pupilla in ipsum spectans contractissima efficiatur. Nempe ex hoc esse videtur, cur visibilis species ex sole procedens, et per pupillam amplificatam intromissa in retinam, ampliorem in illa sedem occupet, majoremque proinde creet solis apparentiam, quam dum per contractam pupillam eodem intromissa contendit. (Vide *Epist. I de apparente Magnitudine solis humilis et sublimis,* p. 6.) [4]

4 ["Hence the following statement can be made: The horizontal sun when visible to the eye appears larger than when it rises higher, because while it is near the horizon there is a mass of extended vapors, and even of corpuscles, which drive back the rays of the sun so that the eye closes less, and the pupil, as if shaded, grows much larger than when, in case the sun is much higher, loose vapors interfere and the sun grows so bright that the pupil, directed toward it, contracts. From this it is cer-

This solution of Gassendus proceeds on a false principle, viz., that the pupils being enlarged augments the species or image on the fund of the eye.

Thirdly, against what is said in sec. 80 it is objected that the same thing which is so small as scarce to be discerned by a man may appear like a mountain to some small insect; from which it follows that the *minimum visibile* is not equal in respect of all creatures. I answer, if this objection be sounded to the bottom it will be found to mean no more than that the same particle of matter, which is marked to a man by one *minimum visibile,* exhibits to an insect a great number of *minima visibilia.* But this does not prove that one *minimum visibile* of the insect is not equal to one *minimum visibile* of the man. The not distinguishing between the mediate and immediate objects of sight is, I suspect, a cause of misapprehension in this matter.

Some other misinterpretations and difficulties have been made, but in the points they refer to I have endeavored to be so very plain that I know not how to express myself more clearly. All I shall add is that if they who are pleased to criticize on my essay would but read the whole over with some attention, they might be the better able to comprehend my meaning and consequently to judge of my mistakes.

I am informed that soon after the first edition of this treatise a man somewhere near London was made to see, who had been born blind and continued so for about twenty years. Such a

tainly apparent why a visible form proceeding from the sun and dispatched through an enlarged pupil to the retina occupies a larger space on it and therefore creates a greater manifestation of the sun than when, dispatched in the same way, it rushes through a contracted pupil."—I am indebted to my colleague, Professor Elmer G. Suhr, for the translation of this passage.

Note that "Gassendus" refers to the French physicist Pierre Gassendi (1592-1655). The work of his that Berkeley refers to is more fully: *De apparente Magnitudine solis humilis atque sublimis, Epistolae quatuor, in quibus complura physica opticaque Problematur proponuntur et explicantur* (Paris, 1642).]

one may be supposed a proper judge to decide how far some tenets laid down in several places of the foregoing essay are agreeable to truth, and if any curious person has the opportunity of making proper interrogatories to him thereon, I should gladly see my notions either amended or confirmed by experience.[5]

5 [The reference in this paragraph is apparently to the case reported in the *Tatler* of August 16, 1709. The surgeon was Mr. Roger Grant, oculist, his patient William Jones of Newington, aged 20. Berkeley does not refer to this case again, perhaps because it appeared to give little support to his theory. Nevertheless it has its own peculiar interest. The patient's fiancée, not visually attractive, was apprehensive about his losing his love for her. He was moved to declare: "Dear Lydia: If I am to lose by sight the soft pantings which I have always felt when I heard your voice, if I am no more to distinguish the step of her I love when she approaches me, but to change that sweet and frequent pleasure for such an amazement as I knew the little time I lately saw; or if I am to have anything besides which may take from me the sense I have of what appeared most pleasing to me at that time (which apparition it seems was you): pull out these eyes before they lead me to be ungrateful to you or undo myself. I wished for them but to see you; pull them out if they are to make me forget you." Instead Berkeley refers to the celebrated Cheselden Case reported by Cheselden in *Philosophical Transactions of the Royal Society of London* in 1728. This, the first definite answer (however it is to be interpreted) to the question asked by Molyneux of Locke thirty-five years earlier, Berkeley regards as confirmation of his theory and quotes the central part of the report in *Visual Language*, sec. 71. For reference to later cases, see Editor's Commentary, sec. 6, note 23, p. xxxi.]

ALCIPHRON

THE FOURTH DIALOGUE
EXCERPTS

6. *Alciphron.* . . . Upon second thoughts, therefore, and a minute examination of this point, I have found that nothing so much convinces me of the existence of another person as his speaking to me. It is my hearing you talk that, in strict and philosophical truth, is to me the best argument for your being. And this is a peculiar argument, inapplicable to your purpose, for you will not, I suppose, pretend that God speaks to man in the same clear and sensible manner as one man does to another?

7. *Euphranor.* How! Is then the impression of sound so much more evident than that of other senses? Or, if it be, is the voice of man louder than that of thunder?

Alc. Alas! you mistake the point. What I mean is not the sound of speech merely as such, but the arbitrary use of sensible signs, which have no similitude or necessary connection with the things signified; so as by the apposite management of them to suggest and exhibit to my mind an endless variety of things, differing in nature, time, and place; thereby informing me, entertaining me, and directing me how to act, not only with regard to things near and present, but also with regard to things distant and future. No matter whether these signs are pronounced or written; whether they enter by the eye or the ear: they have the same use, and are equally proofs of an intelligent, thinking, designing cause.[1]

Euph. But what if it should appear that God really speaks to man; should this content you?

Alc. I am for admitting no inward speech, no holy instincts, or suggestions of light or spirit. All that, you must know,

1 [Cf. *Essay,* sec. 147; *Visual Language,* sec. 40.]

passes with men of sense for nothing. If you do not make it plain to me that God speaks to men by outward sensible signs, of such sort and in such manner as I have defined, you do nothing.

Euph. But if it shall appear plainly that God speaks to men by the intervention and use of arbitrary, outward, sensible signs, having no resemblance or necessary connection with the things they stand for and suggest; if it shall appear that, by innumerable combinations of these signs, an endless variety of things is discovered and made known to us, and that we are thereby instructed or informed in their different natures; that we are taught and admonished what to shun, and what to pursue, and are directed how to regulate our motions, and how to act with respect to things distant from us, as well in time as place, will this content you?

Alc. It is the very thing I would have you make out, for therein consists the force, and use, and nature of language.

8. *Euph.* Look, Alciphron, do you not see the castle upon yonder hill?

Alc. I do.

Euph. Is it not at a great distance [2] from you?

Alc. It is.

Euph. Tell me, Alciphron, is not distance a line turned endwise to the eye?

Alc. Doubtless.

Euph. And can a line, in that situation, project more than one single point on the bottom of the eye?

Alc. It cannot.

Euph. Therefore the appearance of a long and of a short distance is of the same magnitude, or rather of no magnitude at all, being in all cases one single point.

Alc. It seems so.

Euph. Should it not follow from hence that distance is not immediately perceived by the eye?

Alc. It should.

[2] [Cf. secs. 8, 9 with *Essay*, secs. 2-51 and *Visual Language*, secs. 62-6.]

Euph. Must it not then be perceived by the mediation of some other thing?

Alc. It must.

Euph. To discover what this is, let us examine what alteration there may be in the appearance of the same object, placed at different distances from the eye. Now, I find by experience that when an object is removed still farther and farther off in a direct line from the eye, its visible appearance still grows lesser and fainter; and this change of appearance, being proportional and universal, seems to me to be that by which we apprehend the various degrees of distance.

Alc. I have nothing to object to this.

Euph. But littleness or faintness in their own nature seem to have no necessary connection with greater length of distance?

Alc. I admit this to be true.

Euph. Will it not follow then that they could never suggest it but from experience?

Alc. It will.

Euph. That is to say, we perceive distance not immediately but by mediation of a sign, which has no likeness to it or necessary connection with it, but only suggests it from repeated experience, as words do things.

Alc. Hold, Euphranor: now I think of it, the writers in optics tell us of an angle made by the two optic axes, where they meet in the visible point or object; which angle, the obtuser it is the nearer it shows the object to be, and by how much the acuter, by so much the farther off; and this from a necessary [3] demonstrable connection.

Euph. The mind then finds out the distance of things by geometry?

Alc. It does.

Euph. Should it not follow, therefore, that nobody could see but those who had learned geometry, and knew something of lines and angles?

[3] [From a necessary—I: by a necessary.]

Alc. There is a sort of natural geometry which is got without learning.

Euph. Pray inform me, Alciphron, in order to frame a proof of any kind or deduce one point from another, is it not necessary that I perceive the connection of the premises with the conclusion; and in general, to know one thing by means of another, must I not first know that other thing? When I perceive your meaning by your words, must I not first perceive the words themselves? And must I not know the premises before I infer the conclusion?

Alc. All this is true.

Euph. Whoever, therefore, collects a nearer distance from a wider angle, or a farther distance from an acuter angle, must first perceive the angles themselves. And he who does not perceive those angles can infer nothing from them. Is it so or not?

Alc. It is as you say.

Euph. Ask now the first man you meet whether he perceives or knows anything of those optic angles? or whether he ever thinks about them, or makes any inferences from them, either by natural or artificial geometry? What answer do you think he would make?

Alc. To speak the truth, I believe his answer would be that he knew nothing of these matters.

Euph. It cannot therefore be that men judge of distance by angles: nor, consequently, can there be any force in the argument you drew from thence to prove that distance is perceived by means of something which has a necessary connection with it.

Alc. I agree with you.

9. *Euph.* To me it seems that a man may know whether he perceives a thing or no; and, if he perceives it, whether it be immediately or mediately: and, if mediately, whether by means of something like or unlike, necessarily or arbitrarily connected with it.

Alc. It seems so.

Euph. And is it not certain that distance is perceived only by experience, if it be neither perceived immediately by itself, nor by means of any image, nor of any lines and angles which are like it or have a necessary connection with it?

Alc. It is.

Euph. Does it not seem to follow from what has been said and allowed by you that before all experience a man would not imagine the things he saw were at any distance from him?

Alc. How! Let me see.

Euph. The littleness or faintness of appearance, or any other idea or sensation not necessarily connected with or resembling distance, can no more suggest different degrees of distance or any distance at all to the mind which has not experienced a connection of the things signifying and signified than words can suggest notions before a man has learned the language.

Alc. I allow this to be true.

Euph. Will it not thence follow that a man born blind and made to see would, upon first receiving his sight, take the things he saw not to be at any distance from him, but in his eye, or rather in his mind?

Alc. I must own it seems so. And yet, on the other hand, I can hardly persuade myself that if I were in such a state I should think those objects which I now see at so great a distance [4] to be at no distance at all.

Euph. It seems, then, that you now think the objects of sight are at a distance from you?

Alc. Doubtless I do. Can anyone question but yonder castle is at a great distance?

Euph. Tell me, Alciphron, can you discern the doors, windows, and battlements of that same castle?

Alc. I cannot. At this distance it seems only a small round tower.

Euph. But I, who have been at it, know that it is no small round tower, but a large square building with battlements and turrets, which it seems you do not see.

Alc. What will you infer from thence?

4 [So great a distance—I, II: so great distance.]

Euph. I would infer that the very object which you strictly and properly perceive by sight is not that thing which is several miles distant.

Alc. Why so?

Euph. Because a little round object is one thing, and a great square object is another. Is it not?

Alc. I cannot deny it.

Euph. Tell me, is not the visible appearance alone the proper object of sight?

Alc. It is.

What think you now (said *Euphranor,* pointing toward the heavens) of the visible appearance of yonder planet? Is it not a round luminous flat, no bigger than a sixpence?

Alc. What then?

Euph. Tell me then, what you think of the planet itself. Do you not conceive it to be a vast opaque globe, with several unequal risings and valleys?

Alc. I do.

Euph. How can you therefore conclude that the proper object of your sight exists at a distance?

Alc. I confess I know not.

Euph. For your further conviction, do but consider that crimson cloud. Think you that if you were in the very place where it is you would perceive anything like what you now see?

Alc. By no means. I should perceive only a dark mist.

Euph. Is it not plain, therefore, that neither the castle, the planet, nor the cloud which you see here are those real ones which you suppose exist at a distance?

10. *Alc.* What am I to think then? Do we see anything at all, or is it altogether fancy and illusion?

Euph. Upon the whole, it seems the proper objects of sight are light and colors, with their several shades and degrees; all which, being infinitely diversified and combined, form [5] a language wonderfully adapted to suggest and exhibit to us the distances, figures, situations, dimensions, and various qualities

[5] [Form—I: do form.]

of tangible objects: not by similitude,[6] nor yet by inference of necessary connection, but by the arbitrary imposition of Providence, just as words suggest the things signified by them.

Alc. How! Do we not, strictly speaking, perceive by sight such things as trees, houses, men, rivers, and the like?

Euph. We do, indeed, perceive or apprehend those things by the faculty of sight. But will it follow from thence that they are the proper and immediate objects of sight, any more than that all those things are the proper and immediate objects of hearing which are signified by the help of words or sounds?

Alc. You would have us think, then, that light, shades, and colors, variously combined, answer to the several articulations of sound in language; and that, by means thereof, all sorts of objects are suggested to the mind through the eye, in the same manner as they are suggested by words or sounds through the ear: that is, neither from necessary deduction to the judgment, nor from similitude to the fancy, but purely and solely from experience, custom, and habit.

Euph. I would not have you think anything more than the nature of things obliges you to think, nor submit in the least to my judgment, but only to the force of truth, which is an imposition that I suppose the freest thinkers will not pretend to be exempt from.

Alc. You have led me, it seems, step by step, till I am got I know not where. But I shall try to get out again, if not by the way I came, yet by some other of my own finding.

Here *Alciphron,* having made a short pause, proceeded as follows:

11. Answer me, Euphranor, should it not follow from these principles that a man born blind and made to see would, at first sight, not only not perceive their distance, but also not so much as know the very things themselves which he saw, for instance, men or trees? which surely to suppose must be absurd.

Euph. I grant, in consequence of those principles, which

6 [Cf. secs. 10-12 with *Essay,* secs. 121-46 and *Visual Language,* secs. 41-6.]

both of you and I have admitted, that such a one would never think of men, trees, or any other objects that he had been accustomed to perceive by touch, upon having his mind filled with new sensations of light and colors, whose various combinations he does not yet understand, or know the meaning of; no more than a Chinese, upon first hearing the words "man" and "tree," would think of the things signified by them. In both cases, there must be time and experience, by repeated acts, to acquire a habit of knowing the connection between the signs and things signified; that is to say, of understanding the language, whether of the eyes or of the ears. And I conceive no absurdity in all this.

Alc. I see, therefore, in strict philosophical truth, that rock only in the same sense that I may be said to hear it, when the word "rock" is pronounced.

Euph. In the very same.

Alc. How comes it to pass then that every one shall say he sees, for instance, a rock or a house, when those things are before his eyes, but nobody will say he hears a rock or a house, but only the words or sounds themselves by which those things are said to be signified or suggested but not heard? Besides, if vision be only a language speaking to the eyes, it may be asked, when did men learn this language? To acquire the knowledge of so many signs as go to the making up a language is a work of some difficulty. But will any man say he has spent time or been at pains to learn this language of vision?

Euph. No wonder; we cannot assign a time beyond our remotest memory. If we have been all practicing this language, ever since our first entrance into the world; if the Author of nature constantly speaks to the eyes of all mankind, even in their earliest infancy, whenever the eyes are open in the light, whether alone or in company; it does not seem to me at all strange that men should not be aware they had ever learned a language begun so early and practiced so constantly as this of vision. And, if we also consider that it is the same throughout the whole world, and not, like other languages, differing in different places, it will not seem unaccountable that men should mistake the connection between the proper objects of

sight and the things signified by them to be founded in necessary relation or likeness, or that they should even take them
for the same things. Hence it seems easy to conceive why men
who do not think should confound in this language of vision
the signs with the things signified, otherwise than they are
wont to do in the various particular languages formed by the
several nations of men.

12. [*Euph.*] It may be also worth while to observe that,
signs being little considered in themselves or for their own
sake but only in their relative capacity and for the sake of
those things whereof they are signs, it comes to pass that the
mind often overlooks them, so as to carry its attention immediately on to the things signified. Thus, for example, in
reading we run over the characters with the slightest regard,
and pass on to the meaning. Hence it is frequent for men to
say they see words, and notions, and things in reading of a
book; whereas in strictness they see only the characters which
suggest words, notions, and things. And, by parity of reason,
may we not suppose that men, not resting in but overlooking
the immediate and proper objects of sight as in their own
nature of small moment, carry their attention onward to the
very thing signified,[7] and talk as if they saw the secondary
objects? which, in truth and and strictness, are not seen, but
only suggested and apprehended by means of the proper objects of sight, which alone are seen.

Alc. To speak my mind freely, this dissertation grows
tedious, and runs into points too dry and minute for a gentleman's attention.

I thought, said *Crito*, we had been told that minute philosophers loved to consider things closely and minutely.

Alc. That is true, but in so polite an age who would be a
mere philosopher? There is a cerain scholastic accuracy which
ill suits the freedom and ease of a well-bred man. But, to cut
short this chicane, I propound it fairly to your own conscience,
whether you really think that God himself speaks every day
and in every place to the eyes of all men.

---

7 [Thing signified—I, II: things signified.]

Euph. That is really and in truth my opinion, and it should be yours too, if you are consistent with yourself, and abide by your own definition of language. Since you cannot deny that the great Mover and Author of nature constantly explains himself to the eyes of men by the sensible intervention of arbitrary signs which have no similitude or connection with the things signified, so as, by compounding and disposing them, to suggest and exhibit an endless variety of objects differing in nature, time, and place; thereby informing and directing men how to act with respect to things distant and future, as well as near and present. In consequence, I say, of your own sentiments and concessions, you have as much reason to think the Universal Agent or God speaks to your eyes, as you can have for thinking any particular person speaks to your ears.

Alc. I cannot help thinking that some fallacy runs throughout this whole ratiocination, though perhaps I may not readily point it out.[8] It seems to me that every other sense may as well be deemed a language as that of vision. Smells and tastes, for instance, are signs that inform us of other qualities to which they have neither likeness nor necessary connection.

Euph. That they are signs is certain, as also that language and all other signs agree in the general nature of sign, or so far forth as signs. But it is as certain that all signs are not language, not even all significant sounds, such as the natural cries of animals, or the inarticulate sounds and interjections of men. It is the articulation, combination, variety, copiousness, extensive and general use, and easy application of signs (all which are commonly found in vision) that constitute the true nature of language. Other senses may indeed furnish signs, and yet those signs have no more right than inarticulate sounds to be thought a language.

Alc. Hold! Let me see. In language the signs are arbitrary, are they not?

Euph. They are.

Alc. And, consequently, they do not always suggest real

8 [It seems to me. . . . be thought a language. *Alc*. (the remainder of this and the whole of the next paragraph)—Not in I and II.]

matters of fact. Whereas this natural language, as you call it, or these visible signs, do always suggest things in the same uniform way, and have the same constant regular connection with matters of fact: whence it should seem the connection was necessary; and, therefore, according to the definition premised, it can be no language. How do you solve this objection?

Euph. You may solve it yourself by the help of a picture or looking glass.

Alc. You are in the right. I see there is nothing in it. I know not what else to say to this opinion more than that it is so odd and contrary to my way of thinking that I shall never assent to it.

. . . .

14. *Crito.* . . . I think it plain this optic language [9] has a necessary connection with knowledge, wisdom, and goodness. It is equivalent to a constant creation, betokening an immediate act of power and providence. It cannot be accounted for by mechanical principles, by atoms, attractions, or effluvia. The instantaneous production and reproduction of so many signs, combined, dissolved, transposed, diversified, and adapted to such an endless variety of purposes, ever shifting with the occasions and suited to them, being utterly inexplicable and unaccountable by the laws of motion, by chance, by fate, or the like blind principles, does set forth and testify the immediate operation of a spirit or thinking being; and not merely of a spirit, which every motion or gravitation may possibly infer, but of one wise, good, and provident Spirit, who directs and rules and governs the world. Some philosophers, being convinced of the wisdom and power of the Creator, from the make and contrivance of organized bodies and orderly system of the world, did nevertheless imagine that he left this system with all its parts and contents well adjusted and put in motion, as an artist leaves a clock, to go thenceforward of itself for a certain period.[10] But this visual language

9 [I think it plain this optic language—I: This language.]

10 [See Editor's Commentary, sec. 2, p. xi. Cf. Descartes' *Principles*, Bk. IV, 203; also *A Collection of Papers which passed between the Late*

proves not a Creator merely, but a provident Governor, actually and intimately present, and attentive to all our interests and motions, who watches over our conduct, and takes care of our minutest actions and designs throughout the whole course of our lives, informing, admonishing, and directing incessantly, in a most evident and sensible manner. This is truly wonderful.

Euph. And is it not so, that men should be encompassed by such a wonder, without reflecting on it?

15. [*Euph.*] Something there is of divine and admirable in this language, addressed to our eyes, that may well awaken the mind, and deserve its utmost attention; it is learned with so little pains; it expresses the differences of things so clearly and aptly; it instructs with such facility and dispatch, by one glance of the eye conveying a greater variety of advices, and a more distinct knowledge of things, than could be got by a discourse of several hours. And, while it informs, it amuses and entertains the mind with such singular pleasure and delight. It is of such excellent use in giving a stability and permanency to human discourse, in recording sounds and verse with men of remote ages and countries. And it answers so apposite to the uses and necessities of mankind, informing us more distinctly of those objects whose nearness and magnitude qualify them to be of greatest detriment or benefit to our bodies, and

---

Learned Mr. Leibniz and Dr. Clarke in the years 1715 and 1716 (London, 1717), pp. 3 ff., 28 ff. Leibniz writes: "According to their doctrine [that of Newton and his followers] God must rewind (*remonter*) his clock from time to time; otherwise it would cease to move. He had not enough foresight to make it a perpetual motion. This Machine of God according to them is so imperfect that He is obliged to *clean* it from time to time by an extraordinary concourse, and even to *mend* it, as a clockmaker does his work. . . . According to my opinion, the same force and vigor remains always and passes only from one part of matter to another, agreeable to the laws of nature and the beautiful *pre-established* order. . . . I do not say that the corporeal world is a machine or clock that goes *without interposition* of God, . . . but I maintain that it is a clock that goes *without need of correction.*"]

less exactly in proportion as their littleness or distance makes them of less concern to us.

Alc. And yet these strange things affect men but little.

Euph. But they are not strange, they are familiar, and that makes them be overlooked. Things which rarely happen strike, whereas frequency lessens the admiration of things, though in themselves ever so admirable. Hence, a common man, who is not used to think and make reflections, would probably be more convinced of the being of a God by one single sentence heard once in his life from the sky than by all the experience he has had of this visual language, contrived with such exquisite skill, so constantly addressed to his eyes, and so plainly declaring the nearness, wisdom, and providence of Him with whom we have to do.

Alc. After all, I cannot satisfy myself how men should be so little surprised or amazed about this visive faculty, if it was really of a nature so surprising and amazing.

Euph. But let us suppose a nation of men blind from their infancy, among whom a stranger arrives, the only man who can see in all the country; [11] let us suppose this stranger traveling with some of the natives, and that one while he foretells to them that, in case they walk straight forward, in half an hour they shall meet men or cattle, or come to a house; that, if they turn to the right and proceed, they shall in a few minutes be in danger of falling down a precipice; that, shaping their course to the left, they will in such a time arrive at a river, a wood, or a mountain. What think you? Must they not be infinitely surprised that one who had never been in their country before should know it so much better than themselves? And would not those predictions seem to them as unaccountable and incredible as prophecy to a minute philosopher.

Alc. I cannot deny it.

Euph. But it seems to require intense thought to be able to

[11] [Cf. *Essay,* sec. 148 and H. G. Wells's "The Country of the Blind," *Strand Magazine* (April, 1904), first reprinted in *The Country of the Blind* (London, 1911).]

unravel a prejudice that has been so long forming; to get over
the vulgar error of ideas common to both senses; and so to
distinguish between the objects of sight and touch,[12] which
have grown (if I may so say) blended together in our fancy, as
to be able to suppose ourselves exactly in the state that one of
those men would be in, if he were made to see. And yet this
I believe is possible, and might seem worth the pains of a little
thinking, especially to those men whose proper employment
and profession it is to think, and unravel prejudices, and con-
fute mistakes.

Alc. I frankly own I cannot find my way out of this maze,
and should gladly be set right by those who see better than
myself.

Cri. The pursuing this subject in their own thoughts would
possibly open a new scene to those speculative gentlemen of
the minute philosophy. It puts me in mind of a passage in the
Psalmist, where he represents God to be covered with light
as with a garment, and would methinks be no ill comment on
that ancient notion of some Eastern sages—that God had light
for His body and truth for His soul.

This conversation lasted till a servant came to tell us the
tea was ready, upon which we walked in, and found Lysicles
at the tea table.

[12] [Sight and touch—I and II have footnote: See the annexed treatise,
wherein this point and the whole theory of vision are more fully explained. Edition II adds: the paradoxes of which theory, though at first
received with great ridicule by those who think ridicule the test of truth,
were many years after surprisingly confirmed by a case of a person made
to see who had been blind from his birth. See *Phil. Trans.*, No. 402.]

THE THEORY OF VISION

OR

VISUAL LANGUAGE

SHOWING THE IMMEDIATE PRESENCE AND
PROVIDENCE OF A DEITY,

VINDICATED AND EXPLAINED

Acts 17:28
In him we live, and move, and have our being.

A LETTER FROM AN ANONYMOUS WRITER TO THE
AUTHOR OF THE *Minute Philosopher* [1]

REVEREND SIR,

I have read over your treatise called *Alciphron,* in which the
freethinkers of the present age, in their various shifted tenets,
are pleasantly, elegantly, and solidly confuted; the style is easy,
the language plain, and the arguments are nervous; but upon

[1] [Berkeley returned to London from America in October, 1731. In
February, 1732 he published *Alciphron, or the Minute Philosopher* with
the *Essay Towards a New Theory of Vision* annexed. The following letter
from an anonymous writer appeared in the *Daily Post-Boy* of September
9, 1732. In reply Berkeley published *The Theory of Vision or Visual
Language* in 1733 with the letter appended. In the following year (on
April 4, 1734) he wrote to his American friend, Samuel Johnson: "Nor
should I have taken notice of that letter about vision, had it not been
printed in a newspaper which gave it course, and spread it throughout
the kingdom. Besides, the theory of vision I found was somewhat obscure
to most people; for which reason I was not displeased at an opportunity
to explain it."]

the treatise annexed thereto, and upon that part where you seem to intimate that vision is the sole language of God, I beg leave to make these few observations, and offer them to yours and your readers' consideration.

1. Whatever it is without that is the cause of any idea within, I call "the object of sense"; the sensations arising from such objects I call "ideas": the objects therefore that cause such sensations are without us, and the ideas within.

2. Had we but one sense, we might be apt to conclude that there were no objects at all without us, but that the whole scene of ideas which passed through the mind arose from its internal operations; but since the same object is the cause of ideas by different senses, thence we infer its existence; but though the object be one and the same, the ideas that it produces in different senses have no manner of similitude with one another. Because,

3. Whatever connection there is betwixt the idea of one sense, and the idea of another, produced by the same object, arises only from experience. To explain this a little familiarly: let us suppose a man to have such an exquisite sense of feeling given him that he could perceive plainly and distinctly the inequality of the surface of two objects, which by its reflecting and refracting the rays of light produces the ideas of colors. At first in the dark, though he plainly perceived a difference by his touch, yet he could not possibly tell which was red and which was white, whereas a little experience would make him feel a color in the dark, as well as see it in the light.

4. The same word in languages stands very often for the object without, and the ideas it produces within, in the several senses. When it stands for any object without, it is the representative of no manner of idea; neither can we possibly have any idea of what is solely without us. Because,

5. Ideas within have no other connection with the objects without than from the frame and make of our bodies, which is by the arbitrary appointment of God; and though we cannot well help imagining that the objects without are some-

thing like our ideas within, yet a new set of senses, or the alteration of the old ones, would soon convince us of our mistake; and though our ideas would then be never so different, yet the objects might be the same.

6. However, in the present situation of affairs, there is an infallible certain connection betwixt the idea and the object; and therefore, when an object produces an idea in one sense, we know, but from experience only, what idea it will produce in another sense.

7. The alteration of an object may produce a different idea in one sense from what it did before, which may not be distinguished by another sense. But where the alteration occasions different ideas in different senses, we may from our infallible experience argue from the idea of one sense to that of the other; so that if a different idea arises in two senses from the alteration of an object either in situation or distance, or any other way, when we have the idea in one sense, we know from use what idea the object so situated will produce in the other.

8. Hence as the operations of nature are always regular and uniform, where the same alteration of the object occasions a smaller difference in the ideas of one sense, and a greater in the other, a curious observer may argue as well from exact observations as if the difference in the ideas was equal, since experience plainly teaches us that a just proportion is observed in the alteration of the ideas of each sense, from the alteration of the object. Within this sphere is confined all the judicious observations and knowledge of mankind. Now from these observations rightly understood and considered, your new theory of vision must in a great measure fall to the ground, and the laws of optics will be found to stand upon the old unshaken bottom. For though our ideas of magnitude and distance in one sense are entirely different from our ideas of magnitude and distance in another, yet we may justly argue from one to the other, as they have one common cause without, of which, as without, we cannot possibly have the faintest idea. The ideas I have of distance and magnitude by feeling

are widely different from the ideas I have of them by seeing; but that something without, which is the cause of all the variety of the ideas within, in one sense, is the cause also of the variety in the other; and as they have a necessary connection with it, we very justly demonstrate from our ideas of feeling of the same object, what will be our ideas in seeing. And though to talk of seeing by tangible angles and tangible lines be, I agree with you, direct nonsense, yet to demonstrate from angles and lines in feeling, to the ideas in seeing that arise from the same common object, is very good sense, and so vice versa. From these observations thus hastily laid together, and a thorough digestion thereof, a great many useful corollaries in all philosophical disputes might be collected. I am,

Your humble Servant, etc.

THE THEORY OF VISION
OR VISUAL LANGUAGE
VINDICATED AND EXPLAINED [2]

IN ANSWER TO AN ANONYMOUS WRITER

1. An ill state of health, which permits me to apply myself
but seldom and by short intervals to any kind of studies
must be my apology, Sir, for not answering your letter [3]
sooner. This would have altogether excused me from a controversy upon points either personal or purely speculative, or
from entering the lists with declaimers whom I leave to the
triumph of their own passions. And indeed, to one of this
character, who contradicts himself and misrepresents me,
what answer can be made more than to desire his readers
not to take his word for what I say, but to use their own eyes,
read, examine, and judge for themselves? And to their common sense I appeal. For such a writer, such an answer may
suffice. But argument, I allow, has a right to be considered
and, where it does not convince, to be opposed with reason.
And being persuaded that the *Theory of Vision,* annexed to
the *Minute Philosopher,* affords to thinking men a new and

2 [For over a century this work was neglected. In 1860, H. V. H. Cowell
rescued it, noting in the preface of his edition, *Theory of Vision, or Visual
Language, showing the Immediate Presence and Providence of a Deity,
Vindicated and Explained, by the author of Alciphron, or the Minute
Philosopher* (Cambridge and London, 1860): " 'Of English philosophers of
the very highest note,' Sir William Hamilton has observed, '(strange to
say!) there are now actually lying unknown to their editors, biographers,
and fellow metaphysicians, published treatises of the highest interest and
importance [as of Cudworth, Berkeley, Collins, etc.].' "
In secs. 1-8 Berkeley connects his theory with the religious situation;
in 9-18 he gives his definitions; in 19-34 he answers the critic; in 35-70 he
presents the theory; and in 71 he records an experiment whose outcome,
he holds, confirms the theory.]

3 Published in the *Daily Post-Boy* of September 9, 1732. [See p. 117.]

unanswerable proof of the existence and immediate operation of God and the constant condescending care of his
providence, I think myself concerned, as well as I am able,
to defend and explain it, at a time wherein atheism has made
a greater progress than some are willing to own, or others
to believe.

2. He who considers that the present avowed enemies of
Christianity began their attacks against it under the specious
pretext of defending the Christian church and its rights,[4]
when he observes the same men pleading for natural religion,
will be tempted to suspect their views and judge of their
sincerity in one case from what they have showed in the
other. Certainly the notion of a watchful, active, intelligent,
free Spirit, with whom we have to do, and in whom we live,
and move, and have our being, is not the most prevailing in
the books and conversation, even of those who are called
"deists." Besides, as their schemes take effect, we may plainly
perceive moral virtue and the religion of nature to decay,
and see, both from reason and experience, that the destroying
of revealed religion must end in atheism or idolatry. It must
be owned, many minute philosophers would not like at present
to be accounted atheists. But how many, twenty years ago, would
have been affronted to be thought infidels who would now
be much more affronted to be thought Christians! As it would
be unjust to charge those with atheism who are not really
tainted with it, so it will be allowed very uncharitable and
imprudent to overlook it in those who are, and suffer such
men, under specious pretexts, to spread their principles, and
in the event, to play the same game with natural religion
that they have done with revealed.

3. It must, without question, shock some innocent admirers
of a certain plausible pretender[5] to deism and natural religion, if a man should say there are strong signatures of

4 [Matthew Tindal, author of *Rights of the Christian Church* . . . (London, 1706), and *Christianity as Old as the Creation* (London, 1730).]

5 [The third Earl of Shaftesbury (1671-1713), author of *Inquiry Concerning Virtue* (London, 1699), and *Moralists* (London, 1709), reprinted in
Characteristics of Men, Manners, Opinions, Times (London, 1711).]

atheism and irreligion in every sense, natural as well as revealed, to be found even in that admired writer; and yet, to
introduce taste instead of duty, to make man a necessary
agent, to deride a future judgment, seem to all intents and
purposes atheistical, or subversive of all religion whatsoever.
And these every attentive reader may plainly discover to be
his principles, although it be not always easy to fix a determinate sense on such a loose and incoherent writer. There
seems to be a certain way of writing, whether good or bad,
tinsel or sterling, sense or nonsense, which, being suited to
that size of understanding that qualifies its owners for the
minute philosophy, does marvelously strike and dazzle those
ingenious men who are by this means conducted they know
not how, and they know not whither. Doubtless that atheist
who gilds and insinuates and, even while he insinuates, dis-
claims his principles, is the likeliest to spread them. What
avails it in the cause of virtue and natural religion to acknowledge the strongest traces of wisdom and power throughout the structure of the universe, if this wisdom is not employed to observe, nor this power to recompense our actions,
if we neither believe ourselves accountable, nor God our
judge?

4. All that is said of a vital principle of order, harmony,
and proportion; all that is said of the natural decorum and
fitness of things; all that is said of taste and enthusiasm, may
well consist and be supposed, without a grain even of natural
religion, without any notion of law or duty, any belief of a
lord or judge, or any religious sense of a God; the contempla-
tion of the mind upon the ideas of beauty, and virtue, and
order, and fitness being one thing, and a sense of religion
another. So long as we admit no principle of good actions but
natural affection, no reward but natural consequences; so long
as we apprehend no judgment, harbor no fears, and cherish
no hopes of a future state, but laugh at all these things, with
the author of the *Characteristics*, and those whom he esteems
the liberal and polished part of mankind,[6] how can we be
said to be religious in any sense? Or what is here that an

6 Shaftesbury, *Characteristics*, Vol. III, Misc. 3, chap. 2.

atheist may not find his account in, as well as a theist? To
what moral purpose might not fate or nature serve as well
as a deity, on such a scheme? And is not this, at bottom, the
amount of all those fair pretenses?

5. Certainly, that atheistical men who hold no principles
of any religion, natural or revealed, are an increasing number, and this too among people of no despicable rank, has
long since been expressly acknowledged [7] by one who will be
allowed a proper judge, even this same plausible pretender
himself to deism and enthusiasm. But if any well-meaning
persons, deluded by artful writers in the minute philosophy,
or wanting the opportunity of an unreserved conversation
with some ingenious men of that sect, should think that
Lysicles [8] has overshot the mark and misrepresented their
principles—to be satisfied of the contrary, they need only cast
an eye on the *Philosophical Dissertation upon Death*,[9] lately
published by a minute philosopher. Perhaps some man of
leisure may think it worthwhile to trace the progress and
unfolding of their principles down from the writer in defense
of the *Rights of the Christian Church*, to this plain dealer,
the admirable author upon *Death*. During which period of
time I think one may observe a laid design gradually to
undermine the belief of the divine attributes and natural
religion; which scheme runs parallel with their gradual, cov-
ert, insincere proceedings, in respect of the Gospel.

6. That atheistical principles have taken deeper root and
are farther spread than most people are apt to imagine will

[7] *Moralists*, Part II, sec. 3.

[8] [One of the two freethinkers in *Alciphron*, Lysicles represents Bernard
Mandeville (1670-1733), author of *The Fable of the Bees or Private Vices
Public Benefits* (London, 1714). The other is Alciphron, who defends
Shaftesbury's view that ethics is autonomous and that moral judgment is
a kind of taste. Berkeley criticizes these views in the second and third
dialogues, respectively. Mandeville replied with *A Letter to Dion*, i.e.,
George Berkeley (London, 1732).]

[9] [*A Philosophical Dissertation upon Death, composed for the Consola-
tion of the Unhappy*, by a Friend of Truth (London, 1732), attributed to
A. Radicati, Count of Passerano.]

be plain to whoever considers that pantheism, materialism, fatalism are nothing but atheism a little disguised; that the notions of Hobbes, Spinoza, Leibniz, and Bayle are relished and applauded; that as they who deny the freedom and immortality of the soul in effect deny its being, even so they do, as to all moral effects and natural religion, deny the being of God, who deny him to be an observer, judge, and rewarder of human actions; that the course of arguing pursued by infidels leads to atheism as well as infidelity.

[An instance of this may be seen in the proceedings of the author [10] of a book entitled *A Discourse of Freethinking, occasioned by the Rise and Growth of a Sect called Freethinkers,* who, having insinuated his infidelity from men's various pretenses and opinions concerning revealed religion, in like manner appears to insinuate his atheism from the differing notions of men concerning the nature and attributes of God, particularly from the opinion of our knowing God by analogy,[11] as it has been misunderstood and misinterpreted by some of late years. Such is the ill effect of untoward defenses and explanations of our faith, and such advantage do incautious friends give its enemies. If there be any modern well-meaning writer [12] who (perhaps from not having con-

[10] [Anthony Collins, whose discourse, appearing in 1713, started a controversy. Berkeley joined in with his essays against the freethinkers in the *Guardian* of that year.—The brackets around this paragraph are Berkeley's.]

[11] See p. 42 of the mentioned book.

[12] [Peter Browne, Provost of Trinity College, Dublin (1699-1710), and later Bishop of Cork and Ross (1710-35), author of *The Procedure, Extent, and Limits of Human Understanding* (London, 1728). This included an attack on the views of William King, Archbishop of Dublin, presented in a sermon, *Divine Predestination and Foreknowledge* (1709). (See Appendix to *Essay* and note 1, p. 98.) According to Berkeley, King "denied there was any more wisdom, goodness, or understanding in God than there were feet or hands, but that all are to be taken in a figurative sense" (Letter to Percival, March 1, 1710). Berkeley criticized both these views on metaphor and analogy in *Alciphron,* Dial. IV, secs. 16-22, although his views were nearer to Browne's. Browne replied in *Things Divine and Supernatural conceived by Analogy with Things Human* (London, 1733). According to Browne, "Metaphor is merely imaginary and

sidered the fifth book of Euclid) writes much of analogy without understanding it, and thereby has slipped his foot into this snare, I wish him to slip it back again and, instead of causing scandal to good men and triumph to atheists, discreetly explain away his first sense, and return to speak of God and his attributes in the style of other Christians, allowing that knowledge and wisdom do, in the proper sense of the words, belong to God, and that we have some notion, though infinitely inadequate, of those divine attributes, yet still more than a man blind from his birth can have of light and colors.]

But to return, if I see it in their writings, if they own it in their conversation, if their ideas imply it, if their ends are not answered but by supposing it, if their leading author has pretended to demonstrate atheism but thought fit to conceal his demonstration from the public; [13] if this was known in their clubs, and yet that author was nevertheless followed, and represented to the world as a believer of natural religion; if these things are so (and I know them to be so), surely what the favorers of their schemes would palliate, it is the duty of others to display and refute.

7. And, although the characters of divinity are large and legible throughout the whole creation to men of plain sense and common understanding, yet it must be considered that we have other adversaries to oppose, other proselytes to make, men prejudiced to false systems and proof against vulgar arguments, who must be dealt with on a different foot. Conceited, metaphysical, disputing men must be paid in another coin; we must show that truth and reason in all shapes are equally against them, except we resolve to give them up, what they are very fond of being thought to engross, all pretensions to philosophy, science, and speculation.

---

arbitrary without any real similitude and correspondence. . . . Analogy (is) founded in the very nature of the things compared" (p. 449). Berkeley did not reply.]

13 [Anthony Collins, probably referred to in the advertisement of *Alciphron* as one who "declared he had found out a demonstration against the being of a God."]

8. Meanwhile, thus much is evident: those good men who shall not care to employ their thoughts on this *Theory of Vision* have no reason to find fault. They are just where they were, being left in full possession of all other arguments for a God, none of which are weakened by this. And as for those who shall be at the pains to examine and consider this subject, it is hoped they may be pleased to find, in an age wherein so many schemes of atheism are restored or invented, a new argument of a singular nature in proof of the immediate care and providence of a God, present to our minds and directing our actions. As these considerations convince me that I cannot employ myself more usefully than in contributing to awaken and possess men with a thorough sense of the Deity inspecting, concurring, and interesting itself in human actions and affairs, so, I hope, it will not be disagreeable to you that in order to this I make my appeal to reason, from your remarks upon what I have written concerning vision; since men who differ in the means may yet agree in the end, and in the same candor and love of truth.

9. By a sensible object I understand that which is properly perceived by sense. Things properly perceived by sense are immediately perceived. Beside things properly and immediately perceived by any sense, there may be also other things suggested to the mind by means of those proper and immediate objects. Which things so suggested are not objects of that sense, being in truth only objects of the imagination, and originally belonging to some other sense or faculty. Thus sounds are the proper object of hearing, being properly and immediately perceived by that, and by no other sense. But, by the mediation of sounds or words all other things may be suggested to the mind, and yet things so suggested are not thought the object of hearing.

10. The peculiar objects of each sense, although they are truly or strictly perceived by that sense alone, may yet be suggested to the imagination by some other sense. The objects, therefore, of all the senses may become objects of imagination, which faculty represents all sensible things. A color,

therefore, which is truly perceived by sight alone may nevertheless upon hearing the words "blue" or "red" be apprehended by the imagination. It is in a primary and peculiar manner the object of sight; in a secondary manner it is the object of imagination, but cannot properly be supposed the object of hearing.

11. The objects of sense, being things immediately perceived, are otherwise called ideas. The cause of these ideas, or the power producing them, is not the object of sense, not being itself perceived but only inferred by reason from its effects, to wit, those objects or ideas which are perceived by sense. From our ideas of sense the inference of reason is good to a power, cause, agent. But we may not therefore infer that our ideas are like unto this power, cause, or active being. On the contrary, it seems evident that an idea can be only like another idea, and that in our ideas or immediate objects of sense there is nothing of power, causality, or agency included.[14]

12. Hence it follows that the power or cause of ideas is not an object of sense, but of reason. Our knowledge of the cause is measured by the effect of the power by our idea. To the absolute nature, therefore, of outward causes or powers, we have nothing to say; they are no objects of our sense or perception. Whenever, therefore, the appellation of "sensible object" is used in a determined intelligible sense, it is not applied to signify the absolutely existing outward cause or power, but the ideas themselves produced thereby.

13. Ideas, which are observed to be connected together, are vulgarly considered under the relation of cause and effect, whereas, in strict and philosophic truth, they are only related as the sign to the thing signified. For we know our ideas, and therefore know that one idea cannot be the cause of another. We know that our ideas of sense are not the cause of themselves. We know also that we do not cause them. Hence we know they must have some other efficient cause distinct from them and us.[15]

14 [Cf. *Principles*, secs. 25-28.]
15 [Cf. *Principles*, sec. 29.]

14. In treating of vision, it was my purpose to consider the effects and appearances, the objects perceived by my senses, the ideas of sight as connected with those of touch; to inquire how one idea comes to suggest another belonging to a different sense, how things visible suggest things tangible, how present things suggest things remote and future, whether by likeness, by necessary connection, by geometrical inference, or by arbitrary institution.

15. It has indeed been a prevailing opinion and undoubted principle among mathematicians and philosophers that there were certain ideas common to both senses, whence arose the distinction of primary and secondary qualities. But I think it has been demonstrated that there is no such thing as a common object, as an idea, or kind of idea perceived both by sight and touch.[16]

16. In order to treat with due exactness on the nature of vision, it is necessary in the first place accurately to consider our own ideas; to distinguish where there is a difference; to call things by their right names; to define terms, and not confound ourselves and others by their ambiguous use—the want or neglect whereof has so often produced mistakes. Hence it is that men talk as if one idea was the efficient cause of another; hence they mistake inferences of reason for perceptions of sense; hence they confound the power residing in somewhat external with the proper object of sense, which is in truth no more than our own idea.

17. When we have well understood and considered the nature of vision, we may, by reasoning from thence, be better able to collect some knowledge of the external, unseen cause of our ideas, whether it be one or many, intelligent or unintelligent, active or inert, body or spirit. But, in order to understand and comprehend this theory and discover the true principles thereof, we should consider the likeliest way is not to attend to unknown substances, external causes, agents, or powers, nor to reason or infer anything about or from things obscure, unperceived, and altogether unknown.

18. As in this inquiry we are concerned with what objects

16 *Theory of Vision*, secs. 127 ff.

we perceive, or our own ideas, so upon them our reasonings must proceed. To treat of things utterly unknown as if we knew them and so lay our beginning in obscurity, would not surely seem the properest means for the discovering of truth. Hence it follows that it would be wrong, if one about to treat of the nature of vision should, instead of attending to visible ideas, define the object of sight to be that obscure cause, that invisible power or agent, which produced visible ideas in our minds. Certainly, such cause or power does not seem to be the object either of the sense or the science of vision, inasmuch as what we know thereby we know only of the effects. Having premised thus much, I now proceed to consider the principles laid down in your letter, which I shall take in order as they lie.

19. In your first paragraph or section you say that "whatever it is without which is the cause of any idea within, you call 'the object of sense.'" And you tell us soon after this [17] "that we cannot possibly have an idea of any object without." Hence it follows that by an object of sense you mean something that we can have no manner of idea of. This making the objects of sense to be things utterly insensible, or unperceivable, seems to me contrary to common sense, and the use of language. That there is nothing in the reason of things to justify such a definition is, I think, plain from what has been premised; [18] and that it is contrary to received custom and opinion, I appeal to the experience of the first man you meet who, I suppose, will tell you that by an object of sense he means that which is perceived by sense, and not a thing utterly unperceivable and unknown. The beings, substances, powers which exist without may indeed concern a treatise on some other science and may there become a proper subject of inquiry. But why they should be considered as objects of the visive faculty in a treatise of optics, I do not comprehend.

20. The real objects of sight we see, and what we see we know. And these true objects of sense and knowledge, to wit, our own ideas, are to be considered, compared, distinguished

17 Sec. 4.
18 *Supra*, secs. 9, 11, 12.

in order to understand the true theory of vision. As to the outward cause of these ideas, whether it be one and the same, or various and manifold, whether it be thinking or unthinking, spirit or body, or whatever else we conceive or determine about it, the visible appearances do not alter their nature, our ideas are still the same. Though I may have an erroneous notion of the cause, or though I may be utterly ignorant of its nature, yet this does not hinder my making true and certain judgments about my ideas: my knowing which are the same and which different; wherein they agree, and wherein they disagree; which are connected together, and wherein this connection consists: whether it be founded in a likeness of nature, in a geometrical necessity, or merely in experience and custom.

21. In your second section you say "that if we had but one sense, we might be apt to conclude there were no objects at all without us, but that since the same object is the cause of ideas by different senses, thence we infer its existence." Now in the first place I observe that I am at a loss concerning the point which is here assumed, and would fain be informed how we come to know that the same object causes ideas by different senses. In the next place I must observe that, if I had only one sense, I should nevertheless infer and conclude there was some cause without me (which you, it seems, define to be an object) producing the sensations or ideas perceived by that sense. For, if I am conscious that I do not cause them, and know that they are not the cause of themselves, both which points seem very clear, it plainly follows that there must be some other third cause distinct from me and them.

22. In your third section you acknowledge with me "that the connection between ideas of different senses arises only from experience." Herein we are agreed. In your fourth section you say "that a word denoting an external object is the representative of no manner of idea; neither can we possibly have an idea of what is solely without us." What is here said of an external unknown object has been already considered.[19]

19 *Supra*, sec. 19.

23. In the following section of your letter you declare "that our ideas have only an arbitrary connection with outward objects; that they are nothing like the outward objects; and that a variation in our ideas does not imply or infer a change in the objects which may still remain the same." Now, to say nothing about the confused use of the word "object" which has been more than once already observed, I shall only remark that the points asserted in this section do not seem to consist with some others that follow.

24. For in the sixth section you say "that in the present situation of things, there is an infallible certain connection between the idea and the object." But how can we perceive this connection, since according to you [20] we never perceive such object, nor can have any idea of it? Or not perceiving it, how can we know this connection to be infallibly certain?

25. In the seventh section it is said "that we may from our infallible experience argue from our idea of one sense to that of another." But, I think it is plain that our experience of the connection between ideas of sight and touch is not infallible since, if it were, there could be no *deceptio visus* [21] neither in painting, perspective, dioptrics, nor any other wise.

26. In the last section you affirm "that experience plainly teaches us that a just proportion is observed in the alteration of the ideas of each sense, from the alteration of the object." Now I cannot possibly reconcile this section with the fifth, or comprehend how experience should show us that the alteration of the object produces a proportionable alteration, in the ideas of different senses; or how, indeed, it should show us anything at all, either from or about the alteration of an object utterly unknown, of which we neither have nor can have any manner of idea. What I do not perceive or know, how can I perceive, or know to be altered? And, knowing nothing of its alterations, how can I compute anything by them, deduce anything from them, or be said to have any experience about them?

20 *Letter,* sec. 4.
21 [Cf. *Essay,* sec. 45; *Alciphron,* Dial. IV, sec. 12.]

27. From the observations you have premised, rightly understood and considered, you say it follows "that my *New Theory of Vision* must in a great measure fall to the ground; and the laws of optics will be found to stand upon the old unshaken bottom." But, though I have considered and endeavored to understand your remarks, yet I do not in the least comprehend how this conclusion can be inferred from them. The reason you assign for such inference is, "because, though our ideas in one sense are entirely different from our ideas in another, yet we may justly argue from one to the other, as they have one common cause without, of which, you say, we cannot possibly have even the faintest idea." Now my theory nowhere supposes that we may not justly argue from the ideas of one sense to those of another, by analogy and by experience; on the contrary, this very point is affirmed, proved, or supposed throughout.[22]

28. Indeed, I do not see how the inferences which we make from visible to tangible ideas include any consideration of one common, unknown, external cause, or depend thereon, but only on mere custom or habit. The experience which I have had, that certain ideas of one sense are attended or connected with certain ideas of a different sense is, I think, a sufficient reason why the one may suggest the other.

29. In the next place you affirm "that something without, which is the cause of all the variety of ideas within, in one sense, is the cause also of the variety in another; and as they have a necessary connection with it, we very justly demonstrate from our ideas of feeling of the same object, that will be our ideas of seeing." As to which give me leave to remark that to inquire whether that unknown something be the same in both cases, or different, is a point foreign to optics, inasmuch as our perceptions, by the visive faculty, will be the very same, however we determine that point. Perhaps I think that the same Being which causes our ideas of sight causes not only our ideas of touch likewise, but also all our ideas

---

[22] *Theory of Vision,* secs. 38, 78, etc.

of all the other senses, with all the varieties thereof. But this, I say, is foreign to the purpose.

30. As to what you advance, that our ideas have a necessary connection with such cause, it seems to me *gratis dictum:* no reason is produced for this assertion, and I cannot assent to it without a reason. The ideas or effects, I grant, are evidently perceived, but the cause, you say, is utterly unkown.[23] How, therefore, can you tell whether such unknown cause acts arbitrarily or necessarily? I see the effects or appearances; and I know that effects must have a cause; but I neither see nor know that their connection with that cause is necessary. Whatever there may be, I am sure I see no such necessary connection, nor, consequently, can demonstrate by means thereof, from ideas of one sense to those of another.

31. You add that although to talk of seeing by tangible angles and lines be direct nonsense, yet, to demonstrate from angles and lines in feeling, to the ideas in seeing that arise from the same common object, is very good sense. If by this no more is meant than that men might argue and compute geometrically by lines and angles in optics, it is so far from carrying in it any opposition to my theory that I have expressly declared the same thing.[24] This doctrine, as admitted by me, is indeed subject to certain limitations, there being divers cases wherein the writers of optics thought we judged by lines and angles, or by a sort of natural geometry; with regard to which I think they were mistaken, and I have given my reasons for it. And those reasons, as they are untouched in your letter, retain their force with me.

32. I have now gone through your reflections, which the conclusion intimates to have been written in haste, and, having considered them with all the attention I am master of, must now leave it to the thinking reader to judge whether they contain anything that should oblige me to depart from what I have advanced in my *Theory of Vision.* For my own part, if I were ever so willing, it is not on this occasion in my

23 *Letter,* secs. 1, 4.
24 *Theory of Vision,* sec. 78.

power to indulge myself in the honest satisfaction it would be frankly to give up a known error, a thing so much more right and reputable to renounce than to defend. On the contrary, it should seem that the theory will stand secure. Since you agree with me that men do not see by lines and angles. Since I on the other hand agree with you that we may, nevertheless, compute in optics by lines and angles, as I have expressly shown. Since all that is said in your letter about the object, the same object, the alteration of the object, is quite foreign to the theory, which considers our ideas as the object of sense, and has nothing to do with that unknown, unperceived, unintelligible thing, which you signify by the word "object." [25] Certainly, the laws of optics will not stand on the old unshaken bottom, if it be allowed that we do not see by geometry.[26] If it be evident that explications of phenomena given by the received theories in optics are insufficient and faulty. If other principles are found necessary for explaining the nature of vision. If there be no idea nor kind of idea common to both senses,[27] contrary to the old received universal supposition of optic writers.

33. We not only impose on others, but often on ourselves, by the unsteady or ambiguous use of terms. One would imagine that an object should be perceived. I must own when that word is employed in a different sense that I am at a loss for its meaning, and consequently cannot comprehend any arguments or conclusions about it. And I am not sure that, on my own part, some inaccuracy of expression, as well as the peculiar nature of the subject, not always easy either to explain or to conceive, may not have rendered my treatise concerning vision difficult to a cursory reader. But to one of due attention, and who makes my words an occasion of his own thinking, I conceive the whole to be very intelligible. And when it is rightly understood, I scarce doubt but it will be assented to. One thing at least I can affirm, that, if I am mis-

25 *Supra*, sec. 14.
26 *Letter*, sec. 8.
27 *Theory of Vision*. sec. 127.

taken, I can plead neither haste nor inattention, having taken true pains and much thought about it.

34. And had you, Sir, thought it worthwhile to have dwelt more particularly on the subject, to have pointed out distinct passages in my treatise, to have answered any of my objections to the received notions, refuted any of my arguments in behalf of mine, or made a particular application of your own—I might without doubt have profited by your reflections. But it seems to me we have been considering either different things or else the same things in such different views as the one can cast no light on the other. I shall, nevertheless, take this opportunity to make a review of my theory, in order to render it more easy and clear; and the rather because, as I had applied myself betimes to this subject, it became familiar; and, in treating of things familiar to ourselves, we are too apt to think them so to others.

35. It seemed proper, if not unavoidable, to begin in the accustomed style of optic writers, admitting divers things as true which in a rigorous sense are not such, but only received by the vulgar and admitted for such. There has been a long and close connection in our minds between the ideas of sight and touch. Hence they are considered as one thing, which prejudice suits well enough with the purposes of life, and language is suited to this prejudice. The work of science and speculation is to unravel our prejudices and mistakes, untwisting the closest connections, distinguishing things that are different, instead of confused and perplexed, giving us distinct views, gradually correcting our judgment, and reducing it to a philosophical exactness. And, as this work is the work of time, and done by degrees, it is extremely difficult, if at all possible, to escape the snares of popular language and the being betrayed thereby to say things, strictly speaking, neither true nor consistent. This makes thought and candor more especially necessary in the reader. For, language being accommodated to the prenotions of men and use of life, it is difficult to express therein the precise truth of things, which is so distant from their use, and so contrary to our prenotions.

36. In the contrivance of vision, as in that of other things, the wisdom of Providence seems to have consulted the operation, rather than the theory, of man; to the former, things are admirably fitted, but, by that very means, the latter is often perplexed. For, as useful as these immediate suggestions and constant connections are to direct our actions, so is our distinguishing between things confounded, and our separating things connected, and as it were blended together, no less necessary to the speculation and knowledge of truth.

37. The knowledge of these connections, relations, and differences of things visible and tangible, their nature, force, and significancy has not been duly considered by former writers in optics, and seems to have been the great desideratum in that science, which for want thereof was confused and imperfect. A treatise, therefore, of this philosophical kind, for the understanding of vision, is at least as necessary as the physical consideration of the eye, nerve, coats, humors, refractions, bodily nature and motion of light, or the geometrical application of lines and angles for praxis or theory in dioptric glasses and mirrors, for computing and reducing to some rule and measure our judgments, so far as they are proportional to the objects of geometry. In these three lights vision should be considered, in order to be a complete theory of optics.

38. It is to be noted that, in considering the theory of vision, I observed a certain known method [28] wherein, from false and popular suppositions, men do often arrive at truth. Whereas in the synthetical method of delivering science or truth already found, we proceed in an inverted order, the conclusions in the analysis being assumed as principles in the synthesis. I shall therefore now begin with that conclusion, that *vision is the language of the Author of nature,* from thence deducing theorems and solutions of phenomena, and explaining the nature of visible things, and the visive faculty.

39. Ideas, which are observed to be connected with other ideas, come to be considered as signs by means whereof things

---

[28] [Cf. Newton's *Opticks,* Query 31.]

not actually perceived by sense are signified or suggested to the imagination, whose objects they are, and which alone perceives them. And as sounds suggest other things, so characters suggest those sounds; and, in general, all signs suggest the things signified, there being no idea which may not offer to the mind another idea, which has been frequently joined with it. In certain cases a sign may suggest its correlate as an image, in others as an effect, in others as a cause. But where there is no such relation of similitude or causality, nor any necessary connection whatsoever, two things by their mere coexistence, or two ideas, merely by being perceived together, may suggest or signify one the other, their connection being all the while arbitrary; for it is the connection only, as such, that causes this effect.

40. A great number of arbitrary signs, various and apposite, do constitute a language. If such arbitrary connection be instituted by men, it is an artificial language; if by the Author of nature, it is a natural language. Infinitely various are the modifications of light and sound, whence they are each capable of supplying an endless variety of signs and, accordingly, have been each employed to form languages; the one by the arbitrary appointment of mankind, the other by that of God himself.[29] A connection established by the Author of nature, in the ordinary course of things, may surely be called natural, as that made by men will be named artificial. And yet this does not hinder but the one may be as arbitrary as the other. And in fact, there is no more likeness to exhibit or necessity to infer things tangible from the modifications of light, than there is in language to collect the meaning from the sound.[30] But, such as the connection is of the various tones and articulations of voice with their several meanings, the same is it between the various modes of light and their respective correlates, or in other words, between the ideas of sight and touch.

41. As to light, and its several modes or colors, all thinking men are agreed that they are ideas peculiar only to sight;

29 *Minute Philosopher* [*Alciphron*], Dial. IV, secs. 7, 11.
30 *Theory of Vision*, secs. 144, 147.

neither common to the touch, nor of the same kind with any that are perceived by that sense. But herein lies the mistake, that beside these there are supposed other ideas common to both senses, being equally perceived by sight and touch, such as extension, size, figure, and motion. But that there are in reality no such common ideas, and that the objects of sight, marked by those words, are entirely different and heterogeneous from whatever is the object of feeling, marked by the same names, has been proved in the *Theory*,[31] and seems by you admitted. Though I cannot conceive how you should in reason admit this and at the same time contend for the received theories, which are as much ruined as mine is established, by this main part and pillar thereof.

42. To perceive is one thing; to judge is another. So likewise to be suggested is one thing, and to be inferred another. Things are suggested and perceived by sense. We make judgments and inferences by the understanding. What we immediately and properly perceive by sight is its primary object, light and colors. What is suggested or perceived by mediation thereof are tangible ideas, which may be considered as secondary and improper objects of sight. We infer causes from effects, effects from causes, and properties one from another, where the connection is necessary. But how comes it to pass that we apprehend by the ideas of sight certain other ideas, which neither resemble them, nor cause them, nor are caused by them, nor have any necessary connection with them? The solution of this problem, in its full extent, does comprehend the whole theory of vision. Thus stating of the matter places it on a new foot and in a different light from all preceding theories.

43. To explain how the mind or soul of man simply sees is one thing, and belongs to philosophy. To consider particles as moving in certain lines, rays of light as refracted, or reflected, or crossing, or including angles, is quite another thing, and appertains to geometry. To account for the sense of vision by the

---

31 *Ibid.*, sec. 127.

mechanism of the eye is a third thing, which appertains to anatomy and experiments. These two latter speculations are of use in practice, to assist the defects, and remedy the distempers of sight, agreeably to the natural laws obtaining in this mundane system. But the former theory is that which makes us understand the true nature of vision, considered as a faculty of the soul. Which theory, as I have already observed, may be reduced to this simple question, to wit: How comes it to pass that a set of ideas, altogether different from tangible ideas, should nevertheless suggest them to us, there being no necessary connection between them? To which the proper answer is that this is done in virture of an arbitrary connection, instituted by the Author of nature.

44. The proper immediate object of vision is light, in all its modes and variations, various colors in kind, in degree, in quantity; some lively, others faint; more of some, and less of others; various in their bounds or limits; various in their order and situation. A blind man, when first made to see, might perceive these objects, in which there is an endless variety; but he would neither perceive nor imagine any resemblance or connection between these visible objects and those perceived by feeling.[32] Lights, shades, and colors would suggest nothing to him about bodies hard or soft, rough or smooth; nor would their quantities, limits, or order suggest to him geometrical figures, or extension, or situation, which they must do upon the received supposition that these objects are common to sight and touch.[33]

45. All the various sorts, combinations, quantities, degrees, and dispositions of light and colors, would, upon the first perception thereof, be considered in themselves only, as a new set of sensations or ideas. As they are wholly new and unknown, a man born blind would not, at first sight, give them the names of things formerly known and perceived by his touch. But after some experience he would perceive their connection with tangible things and would, therefore, consider

[32] *Theory of Vision*, secs. 41, 106.
[33] [Cf. *Essay*, sec. 133; *Alciphron*, Dial. IV, sec. 11.]

them as signs, and give them (as is usual in other cases) the same names with the things signified.

46. More and less, greater and smaller, extent, proportion, interval are all found in time, as in space; but it will not therefore follow that these are homogeneous quantities. No more will it follow from the attribution of common names that visible ideas are homogeneous with those of feeling. It is true that terms denoting tangible extension, figure, location, motion, and the like are also applied to denote the quantity, relation, and order of the proper visible objects or ideas of sight. But this proceeds only from experience and analogy. There is a *higher* and *lower* in the notes of music. Men speak in a high or a low key. And this, it is plain, is no more than metaphor or analogy. So likewise to express the order of visible ideas the words "situation," "high" and "low," "up" and "down" are made use of, and their sense, when so applied, is analogical.

47. But in the case of vision we do not rest in a supposed analogy between different and heterogeneous natures. We suppose an identity of nature, or one and the same object common to both senses. And this mistake we are led into, forasmuch as the various motions of the head, upward and downward, to the right and to the left, being attended with a diversity in the visible ideas, it comes to pass that those motions and situations of the head, which in truth are tangible, do confer their own attributes and appellations on visible ideas, wherewith they are connected, and which by that means come to be termed "high" and "low," "right" and "left," and to be marked by other names betokening the modes of position; [34] which, antecedently to such experienced connection, would not have been attributed to them, at least not in the primary and literal sense.

48. From hence we may see how the mind is enabled to discern by sight the situation of distant objects. Those immediate objects whose mutual respect and order come to be ex-

[34] *Theory of Vision,* sec. 99.

pressed by terms relative to tangible place being connected with the real objects of touch. What we say and judge of the one, we say and judge of the other, transferring our thought or apprehension from the signs to the things signified; as it is usual, in hearing or reading a discourse, to overlook the sounds or letters, and instantly pass on to the meaning.[35]

49. But there is a great difficulty relating to the situation of objects, as perceived by sight. For since the pencils of rays issuing from any luminous object do, after their passage through the pupil and their refraction by the crystalline, delineate inverted pictures in the retina, which pictures are supposed [36] the immediate proper objects of sight, how comes it to pass that the objects whereof the pictures are thus inverted do yet seem erect and in their natural situation? For the objects not being perceived otherwise than by their pictures, it should follow that as these are inverted, those should seem so too. But this difficulty, which is inexplicable on all the received principles and theories, admits of a most natural solution, if it be considered that the retina, crystalline, pupil, rays crossing, refracted, and reunited in distinct images, correspondent and similar to the outward objects, are things altogether of a tangible nature.

50. The pictures, so called, being formed by the radius pencils after their above-mentioned crossing and refraction are not so truly pictures as images or figures or projections, tangible figures projected by tangible rays on a tangible retina, which are so far from being the proper objects of sight that they are not at all perceived thereby, being by nature altogether of the tangible kind and apprehended by the imagination alone, when we suppose them actually taken in by the eye. These tangible images on the retina have some resemblance unto the tangible objects from which the rays go forth, and in respect of those objects I grant they are inverted. But then I deny that they are, or can be, the proper immediate objects of sight. This

35 *Min. Phil.* [*Alciphron*], Dial. IV, sec. 12.

36 ["Supposed" does not appear in the text. It was added by Berkeley in the list of errata. Cf. "Let us suppose," *Essay*, sec. 114.]

indeed is vulgarly supposed by the writers of optics; but it is a vulgar error which, being removed, the forementioned difficulty is removed with it, and admits a just and full solution, being shown to arise from a mistake.

51. Pictures, therefore, may be understood in a twofold sense, or as two kinds quite dissimilar and heterogeneous, the one consisting of light, shade, and colors; the other not properly pictures, but images projected on the retina. Accordingly, for distinction, I shall call those "pictures" and these "images." The former are visible and the peculiar objects of sight. The latter are so far otherwise that a man blind from his birth may perfectly imagine, understand, and comprehend them. And here it may not be amiss to observe that figures and motions which cannot be actually felt by us, but only imagined, may nevertheless be esteemed tangible ideas, forasmuch as they are of the same kind with the objects of touch, and as the imagination drew them from that sense.

52. Throughout this whole affair, the mind is wonderfully apt to be deluded by the sudden suggestions of fancy which it confounds with the perceptions of sense, and is prone to mistake a close and habitual connection between the most distinct and different things for an identity of nature.[37] The solution of this knot about inverted images seems the principal point in the whole optic theory, the most difficult perhaps to comprehend but the most deserving of our attention and, when rightly understood, the surest way to lead the mind into a thorough knowledge of the true nature of vision.

53. It is to be noted of those inverted images on the retina that, although they are in kind altogether different from the proper objects of sight or pictures, they may nevertheless be proportional to them; as indeed the most different and heterogeneous things in nature may, for all that, have analogy, and be proportional each to other. And although those images, when the distance is given, should be simply as the radiating surfaces; and although it be consequently allowed that the

[37] *Theory of Vision*, sec. 144.

pictures are in that case proportional to those radiating surfaces, or the tangible real magnitude of things; yet it will not
thence follow that in common sight we perceive or judge of
those tangible real magnitudes simply by the visible magnitudes of the pictures; for therein the distance is not given,
tangible objects being placed at various distances, and the
diameters of the images, to which images the pictures are proportional, are inversely as those distances, which distances are
not immediately perceived by sight.[38] And admitting they
were, it is nevertheless certain that the mind, in apprehending
the magnitudes of tangible objects by sight, does not compute
them by means of the inverse proportion of the distances and
the direct proportion of the pictures. That no such inference
or reasoning attends the common act of seeing, everyone's experience may inform him.

54. To know how we perceive or apprehend by sight the real
magnitude of tangible objects, we must consider the immediate visible objects, and their properties or accidents. These immediate objects are the pictures. These pictures are some more
lively, others more faint. Some are higher, others are lower in
their own order, or peculiar location which, though in truth
quite distinct, and altogether different from that of tangible
objects, has nevertheless a relation and connection with it, and
thence comes to be signified by the same terms, "high," "low,"
and so forth. Now by the greatness of the pictures, their faintness, and their situation, we perceive the magnitude of tangible objects. The greater, the fainter, and the upper pictures
suggesting the greater tangible magnitude.

55. For the better explication of this point, we may suppose a diaphanous plane erected near the eye, perpendicular
to the horizon, and divided into small equal squares.[39] A

38 *Theory of Vision*, sec. 2.

39 [A device sometimes used by painters designed to increase their
awareness of pure shapes and relationships. Cf. Dürer's woodcut of the
painter and his frame reproduced by E. H. Gombrich, in *Art and Illusion;
a Study in the Psychology of Pictorial Representation* (New York, 1960);
J. W. Goethe, in *Poetry and Truth*, Part II, Bk. viii, translated by M. S.

straight line from the eye to the utmost limit of the horizon, passing through this diaphanous plane, will mark a certain point or height to which the horizontal plane, as projected or represented in the perpendicular plane, would rise. The eye sees all the parts and objects in the horizontal plane through certain corresponding squares of the perpendicular diaphanous plane. Those that occupy most squares have a greater visible extension, which is proportional to the squares. But the tangible magnitudes of objects are not judged proportional thereto. For those which are seen through the upper squares shall appear vastly bigger than those seen through the lower squares, though occupying the same or a much greater number of those equal squares in the diaphanous plane.

56. Rays issuing from every point of each part or object in the horizontal plane through the diaphanous plane to the eye do to the imagination exhibit an image of the horizontal plane and all its parts, delineated in the diaphanous plane, and occupying the squares thereof to a certain height, marked out by a right line reaching from the eye to the farthest limit of the horizon. A line drawn through the forementioned height or mark upon the diaphanous plane, and parallel to the horizon, I call "the horizontal line." Every square contains an image of some corresponding part of the horizontal plane. And this entire image we may call "the horizontal image," and the picture answering to it "the horizontal picture." In which representation the upper images suggest much greater magnitudes than the lower. And these images suggesting the greater magnitudes are also fainter as well as upper. Whence it follows that faintness and situation concur with visible magnitude to suggest tangible magnitude. For the truth of all which I appeal to the experience and attention of the reader, who shall add his own reflection to what I have written.

Smith (London, 1908), from Goethe's *Dichtung und Wahrheit* (Berlin, 1879); and Gombrich's *(op. cit.,* p. 305) own example of a grid superimposed on Constable's "Wivenhoe Park." Berkeley's device of the diaphanous plane enables him, among other things, to slow down the movement of interpretation.]

57. It is true, this diaphanous plane, and the images supposed to be projected thereon, are altogether of a tangible nature: [40] but then there are pictures relative to those images, and those pictures have an order among themselves answering to the situation of the images, in respect of which order they are said to be "higher" and "lower." [41] These pictures also are more or less faint, they, and not the images, being in truth the visible objects. Therefore what has been said of the images must in strictness be understood of the corresponding pictures, whose faintness, situation, and magnitude, being immediately perceived by sight, do all three concur in suggesting the magnitude of tangible objects, and this only by an experienced connection.

58. The magnitude of the picture will perhaps be thought by some to have a necessary connection with that of the tangible object or (if not confounded with it), to be at least the sole means of suggesting it. But so far is this from being true, that of two visible pictures equally large, the one, being fainter and upper, shall suggest a hundred times greater tangible magnitude than the other [42] which is an evident proof that we do not judge of the tangible magnitude merely by the visible, but that our judgment or apprehension is to be rated rather by other things, which yet, not being conceived to have so much resemblance with tangible magnitude, may therefore be overlooked.

59. It is further to be observed that, besides this magnitude, situation, and faintness of the pictures, our prenotions concerning the kind, size, shape, and nature of things do concur in suggesting to us their tangible magnitudes. Thus, for instance, a picture equally great, equally faint, and in the very same situation shall, in the shape of a man, suggest a lesser tangible magnitude than it would in the shape of a tower.

60. Where the kind, faintness, and situation of the horizon-

40 *Theory of Vision*, sec. 158.
41 *Supra*, sec. 46.
42 *Theory of Vision*, sec. 78.

tal pictures [43] are given, the suggested tangible magnitude will be as the visible. The distances and magnitudes, that we have been accustomed to measure by experience of touch, lying in the horizontal plain, it thence comes to pass that situations of the horizontal pictures suggest the tangible magnitudes, which are not in like manner suggested by vertical pictures. And it is to be noted that, as an object gradually ascends from the horizon toward the zenith, our judgment concerning its tangible magnitude comes by degrees to depend more entirely on its visible magnitude. For the faintness is lessened as the quantity of intercepted air and vapors is diminished; and as the object rises, the eye of the spectator is also raised above the horizon. So that the two concurring circumstances of faintness and horizontal situation, ceasing to influence the suggestion of tangible magnitude, this same suggestion or judgment does in proportion thereto become the sole effect of the visible magnitude and the prenotions. But it is evident that if several things (for instance, the faintness, situation, and visible magnitude) concur to enlarge an idea, upon the gradual omission of some of those things, the idea will be gradually lessened. This is the case of the moon,[44] when she ascends above the horizon and gradually diminishes her apparent dimension as her altitude increases.

61. It is natural for mathematicians to regard the visual angle and the apparent magnitude as the sole or principal means of our apprehending the tangible magnitude of objects. But it is plain from what has been premised that our apprehension is much more influenced by other things,[45] which have no similitude or necessary connection therewith.

62. And these same means, which suggest the magnitude of tangible things, do also suggest their distance,[46] and in the same manner, that is to say, by experience alone, and not by

---

[43] *Supra*, sec. 56.
[44] *Theory of Vision*, sec. 73.
[45] *Supra*, sec. 58.
[46] *Theory of Vision*, sec. 77.

any necessary connection, or geometrical inference. The faintness, therefore, and vividness, the upper and lower situation, together with the visible size of the pictures, and our prenotions concerning the shape and kind of tangible objects are the true media by which we apprehend the various degrees of tangible distance. Which follows from what has been premised, and will indeed be evident to whoever considers that those visual angles, with their arches or subtenses, are neither perceived by sight nor by experience of any other sense. Whereas it is certain that the pictures, with their magnitudes, situations, and degrees of faintness are alone the proper objects of sight. So that whatever is perceived by sight, must be perceived by means thereof. To which perception the prenotions also, gained by experience of touch or of sight and touch conjunctly, do contribute.

63. And indeed we need only reflect on what we see to be assured that the less the pictures are, the fainter they are, and the higher (provided still they are beneath the horizontal [47] line or its picture) by so much the greater will the distance seem to be. And this upper situation of the picture is in strictness what must be understood when, after a popular manner of speech, the eye is said to perceive fields, lakes, and the like, interjacent [48] between it and the distant object, the pictures corresponding to them being only perceived to be lower than that of the object.[49] Now it is evident that none of these things have in their own nature any necessary connection with the various degrees of distance. It will also appear upon a little reflection that sundry circumstances of shape, color, and kind do influence our judgments or apprehensions of distance—all which follows from our prenotions, which are merely the effect of experience.

64. As it is natural for mathematicians to reduce things to the rule and measure of geometry, they are prone to suppose that the apparent magnitude has a greater share than we

47 *Supra*, sec. 56.
48 *Theory of Vision*, sec. 3.
49 *Supra*, sec. 55.

really find in forming our judgment concerning the distance of things from the eye. And, no doubt, it would be an easy and ready rule to determine the apparent place of an object if we could say that its distance was inversely as the diameter of its apparent magnitude, and so judge by this alone exclusive of every other circumstance. But that this would be no true rule is evident, there being certain cases in vision, by refracted or reflected light, wherein the diminution of the apparent magnitude is attended with an apparent diminution of distance.

65. But further to satisfy us that our judgments or apprehensions, either of the greatness or distance of an object, do not depend absolutely on the apparent magnitude, we need only ask the first painter we meet who, considering nature rather than geometry, well knows that several other circumstances contribute thereto; and since art can only deceive us as it imitates nature, we need but observe pieces of perspective and landscapes to be able to judge of this point.

66. When the object is so near that the interval between the pupils bears some sensible proportion to it, the sensation which attends the turn or straining of the eyes in order to unite the two optic axes therein is to be considered as one means of our perceiving distance.[50] It must be owned, this sensation belongs properly to the sense of feeling; but as it waits upon, and has a constant regular connection with, distinct vision of near distance (the nearer this, the greater that), so it is natural that it should become a sign thereof, and suggest it to the mind.[51] And that it is so in fact follows from that known experiment of hanging up a ring edgewise to the eye and then endeavoring, with one eye shut, by a lateral motion, to insert into it the end of a stick; which is found more difficult to perform than with both eyes open, from the want of this means of judging by the sensation attending the nearer meeting or crossing of the two optic axes.

67. True it is that the mind of man is pleased to observe in nature rules or methods, simple, uniform, general, and re-

50 *Theory of Vision*, sec. 16, 17.
51 *Supra*, sec. 39.

ducible to mathematics, as a means of rendering its knowledge at once easy and extensive. But we must not, for the sake of uniformities or analogies, depart from truth and fact nor imagine that in all cases the apparent place or distance of an object must be suggested by the same means. And, indeed, it answers the ends of vision to suppose that the mind should have certain additional means or helps for judging more accurately of the distance of those objects, which are the nearest, and consequently most concern us.

68. It is also to be observed that when the distance is so small that the breadth of the pupil bears a considerable proportion to it, the object appears confused. And this confusion, being constantly observed in poring on such near objects, and increasing as the distance lessens, becomes thereby a means of suggesting the place of an object.[52] For one idea is qualified to suggest another, merely by being often perceived with it. And if the one increases either directly or inversely as the other, various degrees of the former will suggest various degrees of the latter, by virtue of such habitual connection, and proportional increase or diminution. And thus the gradual changing confusedness of an object may concur to form our apprehension of near distance when we look only with one eye. And this alone may explain Dr. Barrow's difficulty,[53] the case as proposed by him, regarding only one visible point.[54] And when several points are considered, or the image supposed an extended surface, its increasing confusedness will, in that case, concur with the increasing magnitude to diminish its distance, which will be inversely as both.

69. Our experience in vision is got by the naked eye. We apprehend or judge from this same experience when we look through glasses. We may not, nevertheless, in all cases conclude from the one to the other, because that certain circumstances either excluded or added, by the help of glasses, may

52 *Theory of Vision*, sec. 21.
53 [Cf. *Essay*, secs. 29 ff.]
54 *Theory of Vision*, sec. 29.

sometimes alter our judgments, particularly as they depend upon prenotions.

70. What I have here written may serve as a commentary on my *Essay Towards a New Theory of Vision,* and, I believe, will make it plain to thinking men. In an age wherein we hear so much of thinking and reasoning it may seem needless to observe how useful and necessary it is to think, in order to obtain just and accurate notions, to distinguish things that are different, to speak consistently, to know even our own meaning. And yet for want of this we may see many, even in these days, run into perpetual blunders and paralogisms. No friend, therefore, to truth and knowledge, would lay any restraint or discouragement on thinking. There are, it must be owned, certain general maxims, the result of ages and the collected sense of thinking persons, which serve instead of thinking for a guide or rule to the multitude who, not caring to think for themselves, it is fit they should be conducted by the thought of others. But those who set up for themselves, those who depart from the public rule, or those who would reduce them to it, if they do not think, what will men think of them? As I pretend not to make any discoveries which another might not as well have made who should have thought it worth his pains, so I must needs say that without pains and thought no man will ever understand the true nature of vision, or comprehend what I have written concerning it.

71. Before I conclude, it may not be amiss to add the following extract from the *Philosophical Transactions,* relating to a person blind from his infancy, and long after made to see: "When he first saw, he was so far from making any judgment about distances that he thought all objects whatever touched his eyes (as he expressed it) as what he felt did his skin; and thought no objects so agreeable as those which were smooth and regular, though he could form no judgment of their shape, or guess what it was in any object that was pleasing to him. He knew not the shape of any thing, nor any one thing from another, however different in shape or magnitude; but upon

being told what things were, whose form he before knew from feeling, he would carefully observe that he might know them again; but having too many objects to learn at once, he forgot many of them; and (as he said) at first he learned to know, and again forgot a thousand things in a day. Several weeks after he was couched, being deceived by pictures, he asked which was the lying sense, feeling or seeing? He was never able to imagine any lines beyond the bounds he saw. The room he was in, he said, he knew to be but part of the house, yet he could not conceive that the whole house could look bigger. He said every new object was a new delight, and the pleasure was so great that he wanted ways to express it." [55] Thus, by fact and experiment those points of the theory which seem the most remote from common apprehension were not a little confirmed many years after I had been led into the discovery of them by reasoning.

[55] *Phil. Transact.*, No. 402. [This case was reported by Mr. Will Cheselden, F.R.S., in 1728. Berkeley's extract gives the central part of the report. For extracts from other reports, see Editor's Commentary, sec. 6, note 23, p. xxxi. See also M. Von Senden's *Space and Sight*.]

INDEX *

Abbott, Thomas K., 19n
Abstract ideas, xvi, xxxv f., xliii f., 40 f., 141; of extension and Locke's triangle, *Essay*, 122-25
Ambiguity, xxxii f., xl f., 135
Analysis and synthesis, vii f., xv f.; defined, *Visual Language*, 38
"Ancient Principle," xxxviii n; "the most fecund in all catoptrics," 31n; adopted by Tacquet, 31; overthrown by Barrovian Case, 31 f.
"Anti-Berkeley": criticizes Berkeley on *minimum visibile*, 60n
Aristotle, viii, xiv, xxi, xxvii, xxxii, 9n, 72n; sets problem of vision, xix ff.; defines proper object, xix, 4n; offers hint of visual language, xxi; defines metaphor, xxxv
Armstrong, David M., 19n, 96n
Association, xxx, 23 ff., 70, 110, 133, 138
Author of visual language, xxxiv, xlv, 5, 92, 103 f., 112, 137 f., 140

Bacon, Roger, xxii, xxxix n, 32n, 55n
Bailey, Samuel, xviii n, 19n
Barrovian Case, xix, xxxviii, xl f., *Essay*, 29-40, *Visual Language*, 68; solution of, by Lin-

guistic Theory, *Essay*, 31-39, *Visual Language*, 68; and suggested experiment, *Essay*, 36
Barrow, Isaac, xxxviii, xl f., 27 ff., 150; encounters a "certain untoward difficulty" (the Barrovian Case), 29
Bayle, Pierre, 125
Beck, Lewis W., xvii n
Berkeley, Anne, xii n
Blind, country of the, 115
Blind from birth, made to see, 4, 107, 109 f., 140 f., *Essay*, 41, 79, 92-110, 128, 132-37; experiments performed on, ix, xxxi n, 102n, *Visual Language*, 71
Blind with crossed sticks (Descartes' device), xxv, 38, 64 f., 98 f.
Browne, Peter, 125n

Camera model: illustrates the eye, xvi, xxii; illustrates the mind, xvi, xxiv; provides mental vocabulary, xxiv; defects and merits of, xxiv ff.
Cartesian–Newtonian myth. *See* Myth of mechanism
Cassirer, Ernst, xxx n
Cause and effect, 138 f.; signs and things signified mistaken for, *Visual Language*, 13
Cause or power, *Visual Language*, 11-14, 16-21, 28, 29, 30; not an object of sense but of

* In the Index, references to whole sections of the *Essay*, *Visual Language*, etc., are given in boldface numbers.

153

The Library of Liberal Arts